A Grammar of Mode

A Grammar
of Modern English

W. H. MITTINS
Lecturer in Education
University of Newcastle upon Tyne

METHUEN & CO LTD
11 New Fetter Lane EC4

First published *1962* by Methuen & Co Ltd
© *1962* by W. H. Mittins
Reprinted *1964* and *1967*
Printed in Great Britain
by Fletcher & Son Ltd, Norwich

Paperback edition first published *1967*
Reprinted *1970*
Reprinted *1973*

SBN *416 69810 7*

Distributed in the U.S.A. by
HARPER & ROW PUBLISHERS INC
BARNES & NOBLE IMPORT DIVISION

CONTENTS

FOREWORD

FEW teachers of English as a first language would favour the reinstatement of traditional Latinate grammar in the central position it used to occupy in English studies. But a growing number seem to be convinced of the need for a new kind of grammar, oriented towards the language of today as used by responsible speakers and writers. These teachers are handicapped by the lack of textbooks which, in the words of James Sledd, are 'linguistically respectable and pedagogically usable'. Sledd and one or two other Americans have in fact produced textbooks for schools and colleges in the U.S.A. It seems timely to attempt something of the kind in Britain.

A fully 'respectable' teaching-grammar cannot be expected until a complete description of English usage is provided. Professor Randolph Quirk and a London University team are engaged upon such a description, but have years of work yet to do. Meanwhile, those who believe that language-study has an important contribution to make to the teaching of English need interim textbooks incorporating such linguistic findings as are available and relevant.

This book tries to meet that need. It assumes that a realistic study of the grammatical structures of modern English can help users of the language to communicate in it more effectively, more precisely, and more resourcefully than they otherwise might. If, as seems demonstrable, the poor quality of much English speech and writing derives from looseness in verbal construction and reliance upon a

very restricted range of constructions, a systematic
examination of the nature and range of verbal patterns
might conceivably foster both firmness and resourcefulness
in the matching of words to meanings. It is hoped, too,
that the emphasis in the later sections on choosing among
alternative structures (i.e. stylistics) will help towards the
integration of grammar with matters of composition and
literature.

There is probably as much difference of opinion about
the timing as about other aspects of a grammar course. I
have aimed primarily at the upper forms of grammar
schools. It is idle to pretend that English grammar is an
easy subject, but there should be little in the book beyond
the grasp of the average G.C.E. Ordinary Level candidate.
Nevertheless, some teachers might prefer to wait until the
Sixth Form stage.

One of the main differences from conventional school
grammars is the accordance of priority to speech patterns.
The primacy of the spoken language is being increasingly
recognized, and it is hoped that the elementary analysis of
features of intonation in the early chapters will illuminate
important distinctions between speech and writing and
will provide a frame of reference for much of the later
grammatical discussion.

Nomenclature remains a peculiarly intractable problem.
There seems as little uniformity of usage among new as
among traditional grammarians. The most blurred of
traditional terms (e.g. Noun, Adjective) and the most
technical of modern linguistic terms (e.g. morpheme, im-
mediate constituent) have been avoided. Many more or
less satisfactory conventional terms (e.g. Verb, Complement) have been retained. Some familiar labels have been
slightly modified (e.g. Adverbal). And a few comparative
novelties (e.g. Adnominal, Verbid) have been adopted.

The total compromise, if not agreeable, ought at least to prove workable.

'Learning by doing' seems specially appropriate to native language work. This manual is therefore primarily a practical work-book. The comments are kept as short as possible, to encourage concentration on the scrutiny of samples and the working of exercises. The risk of presenting occasional examples of unsatisfactory usage† is deliberately taken where this seems to be the most effective way of making a point. The frequent recourse to newspaper headlines may be thought even more risky, but headlines have two marked advantages. First, by reducing patterns to the barest minimum, they draw attention to basic structures in a most stark way. Secondly, they constitute a rich source of manageable linguistic material readily available to all students and operating (unlike many textbook exemplars) in a real-life context.

W. H. M.

---

† Where these occur as 'samples' they are marked with an asterisk *

ACKNOWLEDGEMENTS

GRATEFUL acknowledgement is made to Bodley Head Ltd. for permission to reproduce excerpts from *How To Write, The Hohenzollerns in America*, and *The Garden of Folly*, by Stephen Leacock; to the Hogarth Press for the excerpts from *Flush*, by Virginia Woolf; and to Victor Gollancz Ltd. for the excerpts from *The Return of Hyman Kaplan*, by Leo Rosten.

Acknowledgement is also due to Ben Traven for the excerpt adapted from *The Treasure of the Sierra Madre* (Hutchinson and Co., [Publishers] Ltd.); to Roy Fuller for the excerpt from *Savage Gold* (Hutchinson and Co., [Publishers] Ltd.); to William Faulkner for the excerpt from *A Fable* (Chatto and Windus Ltd.); to Walter Macken for the excerpt from 'The Lion' from *Winter's Tales 3* (Macmillan and Co., Ltd.); and to Kay Cicellis and the *London Magazine* (June 1960) for the excerpt from the short story *Arise and Eat*.

Part One

MEANING IN SPEECH AND WRITING

---

1 · Meaning and Context

SAMPLE

A] LIFT (Noticeboard alongside elevator shaft)
   'Lift!' shouted the foreman to the gang erecting the telegraph pole.
B] STEP INSIDE
   'Step inside,' invited a pleasant voice.
c] Mrs Gregory was indoors *dusting* the piano, while her husband was in the garden *dusting* the cabbages with insecticide.

COMMENT

A] A word on its own is not meaningful; what it means depends on its context. A word's context includes the words around it, the users of the words (speaker and listener, or writer and reader), the place, the state of affairs, and so on. Thus 'lift' can, according to circumstances, mean 'Here is the elevator' or 'Raise it off the ground!'
B] Similarly 'step inside' might be a warning to beware of the step or an invitation to come in. Only a fuller context can clear up this ambiguity.
c] Here context and our knowledge of ordinary human

behaviour lead us without hesitation to accept the first 'dusting' in the sense of *removing* dust, the second in the contrary sense of *adding* dust.

EXERCISES

1. Suggest for each of the following words two contexts which would give it quite different meanings:

Fire	Press	Up	Out	Off
Halt	Cricket	Home	Private	Players

2. Do the same for the following word-groups:

long sentence	(composition/crime)
last post	(mail/military funeral)
He needed a long rest	(convalescence/billiards)
Take One	(free leaflet/filming)
Indian Braves Fire	(newspaper headline)

3.

COAL STRIKE IN SCOTLAND

OIL STRIKE IN TEXAS

In these two headlines 'strike' has two very different meanings. What circumstances suggest one meaning in the first case, another in the second?

2 · Clusters

SAMPLE

A]

Lunch	lasted	hours.
The midday meal	went on	for a long time.

He *is proposing* to retire soon. (intends)
There was no tree *to be seen* for miles. (visible)

A sailor *with a wooden leg* was singing noisily. (wooden-legged)

Few people are *able to use both hands equally well*. (ambi-dextrous)

You need shoes *that will keep out water*. (waterproof)

B] He was writing the story of his life.

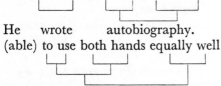

He   wrote   autobiography.

(able) to use both hands equally well

C] (the) fat policeman's wife   (the) fat policeman's wife

D] three times seven plus two:

$$3 \times (7 + 2) = 27 \quad \text{or} \quad (3 \times 7) + 2 = 23$$

COMMENT

A] Most sentences other than the very simplest contain at least one group of words which belong more closely to one another than to other words in the sentence. Such word-groups, which are often more or less equivalent in meaning to single words, may be called *Clusters*.

B] In sizeable sentences containing a number of clusters some clusters belong more closely to each other than to other clusters. In such cases the ranking can be shown by a kind of inverted family tree.

C] Sometimes in writing (though not in speech – see Sections 3–5) the ranking is not clear and two meanings are possible.

D] In mathematics a similar ambiguity is avoided by the use of brackets.

EXERCISES

1. Suggest single words more or less equivalent in meaning to the clusters italicized in:

   a) She *made up her mind* to enter the contest.
   b) *Little by little* the chest sank in the mud.
   c) It was an experience *to be remembered*.
   d) All their efforts were *to no purpose*.
   e) Much of what the speaker said was *off the point*.
   f) A dog *that was* apparently *fierce of disposition* was guarding the gate.
   g) His parents had *left the country in order to live overseas*.
   h) He *said that* the accusation *was untrue*.
   i) Her essay was full of *sentences taken from books*.
   j) It was a situation *we could not put up with*.

2. Treat the following sentences in the same way as in Sample B above. That is, first indicate the smallest clusters by bracketing; then bracket together the clusters progressively.

   a) The city's new Lord Mayor is threatening to resign immediately.
   b) Few people are able to possess everything they want.
   c) The travellers' passports were returned to them.
   d) Several thousand public transport employees suddenly went on unofficial strike.
   e) The result of the election ought to have been declared at midnight.

3. Make up pairs of sentences to illustrate the pairs of possible meanings of:

   a) the former minister's residence
   b) the daughter of the president's son
   c) new members' lounge
   d) more difficult problems
   e) a single woman's job

3 · Speech Patterns – Transition

A] The engine won't start ↘ I'll have to investigate ↘
Perhaps we have run out of petrol ↘ That's what happened last time ↘
How stupid of you ↘ You really ought to know better ↘

B] Won't the engine start ↗ You'll have to investigate ↘
Have we run out of petrol ↗ That's what happened last time ↘
The engine won't start ↗ What a nuisance ↘

C] The engine won't start →↗ but we've plenty of petrol ↘
How stupid of you →↗ you careless dolt ↘
Nobody noticed the number of the car which had been stolen ↘
Nobody noticed the number of the car →↗ which had been stolen ↘

D] Shall I $^{+}$ scream for ice $^{+}$ cream ↗
Fancy bringing a briefcase for such a brief $^{+}$ case ↘

COMMENT

(NOTE: The analysis of speech patterns is a comparatively new study. Experts are by no means agreed on what distinctions can properly be made and on how they may best be shown in writing. In any case, speakers vary in their speech habits. This and the following two sections are intended only as rough guides to one way of treating this important matter.)

Transition is the process of passing from one item (syllable, word, word-group, sentence) to another. Four kinds of

B

'break' or 'holding-on' seem to be distinguishable. The first three (A, B, C) are usually called *terminals*, because they come at the end of segments of speech. The fourth (D) is known variously as *open transition* or *plus juncture*.

A] The falling terminal ↘ characteristically marks the end of a statement or command or exclamation, and often follows a fall in the pitch or level of the voice. It represents a fading away into silence. It commonly coincides with (in writing) the full-stop, semi-colon, or exclamation mark.

B] The rising terminal ↗ characteristically marks the end of a question and often follows a rise in the pitch of the voice. Note, however, that this is not the only way of marking a question; where a question-word (who? how? where? etc.) is used, a question commonly follows the same pattern as the statement: e.g. Who was that ↘.

c] The level terminal → characteristically separates two segments but without any change of pitch. It often corresponds to the written comma. Like it, it can, for instance, mark the distinction between restrictive and non-restrictive clauses, as in the two renderings of the 'Nobody noticed . . .' sentence. (See also Section 40 below.)

D] Plus juncture normally (though by no means invariably) coincides with the division between words.

EXERCISES

1. Read aloud the sentences in the Sample above, observing the terminals and plus junctures marked.
2. Write out a short telephone conversation. Mark the important terminal junctures.
3. Copy out the following sentences. Read each one aloud.

Then underline the pair of contrasted items in it, and put in the important plus junctures.

a) Blackbirds are not the only kind of black birds.
b) A glasshouse is not really a glass house.
c) The loudspeaker need not have been used by such a loud speaker.
d) I see Mabel, but I don't seem able to attract her attention.
e) They freed Annie willingly, but they refused to free Danny.
f) He was in need of a rest and therefore welcomed his arrest.
g) If you show me the market, I'll mark it on my map.
h) He shot an arrow through a narrow crack in the wall.
i) Just leave me that sample; that's ample.
j) The poster urged the public to post early for Christmas.

4 · Speech Patterns – Stress

SAMPLE

A] líghthòusekèepĕr
télĕgràph pôle
meăt-pàste sándwĭch
brĭéfcàse   ă brĭéf cáse   brĭéflў
Gérmăn stûdeʹnt   Gêrmăn stúdeʹnt
B] 1st speaker: How áre you?
2nd speaker: Wéll, thank you. How are yóu?
C] Professor   Rákes → Léaves ↘
Proféssor → Rakes   Léaves ↘
When eating físh → always use a físh-knife ↘

When eating →ˉ fís͏h always use a fís͏h-knife ↘

Alfred stóod →ˉ by his bróther ↘

Alfred stood bý →ˉ his bróther ↘

The wind bléw →ˉ down the chímney ↘

The wind →ˉ blew dówn the chímney ↘

ă + blâckbìrd's + nést

ă + blâck + bírd's-nest

ă + blâck + bîrd's + nést

D] The patient *came tó*. (= recovered consciousness, revived)

It was the very same place we *cáme to*. (= reached)

COMMENT

(See Note at beginning of Comment on Transition, p. 5 above.)

A] Many experts have more or less agreed in distinguishing four degrees of stress:

′ primary

ˆ secondary

ˋ tertiary

ˇ weak

In phrases such as 'German student' the stress pattern is the main clue to difference of meaning, in this case between 'one who studies German' and 'a German-born student'.

B] Variations in the distribution of stress often reflect differences of emphasis and order of speaking in dialogue.

C] Variation in the placing of primary stress can combine with variation in the placing of level transition or of plus juncture to convey very different meanings.

D] Placing of primary stress can mark the important distinction between a Phrasal Verb (see Section 11 below) and a separate Verb with Particle.

EXERCISES

1. Read aloud the examples in the Sample above, observing the stresses and transitions marked.

2. Each of the following four-syllable utterances can be spoken to illustrate the four different stresses. Say them aloud; then write them down and mark the stresses.

a) lighthousekeeper   *f*) cinema seat
b) for a long time   *g*) windscreen washer
c) all of my friends   *h*) hothouse flowers
d) How do we know?   *i*) Is the car there?
e) Where's the bookcase?   *j*) leather suitcase

3. Read aloud the following pairs of sentences. Then write them down and put in the important stresses and transition marks.

a) The wind blew up the lane.
The spy blew up the ammunition dump.
b) Twenty-odd women competed.
Twenty odd women competed.
c) They passed by the other road. (= went by another route)
They passed by the other road. (= overlooked the other road)
d) Have you ever seen a horsefly?
Have you ever seen a horse fly?
e) What are you working for? (= What is your objective?)
What are you working for? (= Why are you working?)

4. Examine Sample D again (came tó/cáme to). Then make up pairs of sentences to show how similar stress variation is possible with each of the following.

a) turned up
b) a fair girl
c) a sound machine
d) a light beam
e) drinking water

5. Example: (Where are you going?)   I'm gôing hóme.
(What are you doing?)   I'm góing hôme.
(What do yóu mean to do?) Í'm gòing hôme.

Show how different stress patterns can give different emphasis to each of the following. Indicate the kind of question each utterance might be answering.

a) He ran away.
b) The committee chose the colours.
c) I'll look after the animals.
d) The headmaster chose the prizes.
e) She collects butterflies.

5 · Speech Patterns – Pitch

SAMPLE

A] ²He's feeling ³tired¹ ↘
²We ³asked her² → ²but she didn't re³ply¹ ↘

B] ²How are ¹you³ ↗ ³Well, ²thanks → ²How are ³you¹ ↘
²Shall we ¹go³ ↗
²Are you ¹there³ ↗

c] ²Where are you ³going¹ ↘ (normal inquiry)
²Where are you ⁴going¹ ↘ (alarm)
²Where ⁴are you ³going¹ ↘ (puzzlement)
²Well, ⁴look who's ⁴here² ↘
²I don't mind ³scoring² → ²but I couldn't ⁴possibly²
³umpire¹ ↘

COMMENT

(See Note at beginning of Comment on Transition, p. 5 above.)

A] A third feature of speech patterns is variation in pitch or level of the voice. Here again four grades have been distinguished. The commonest three – mid(2), high(3), low(1) – occur in that order in the standard pattern of ordinary statements. The mid level(2) is the basic normal level of the voice.

B] Questions frequently use the same pattern, but have a possible 2–1–3 variant with a final upward rise.

c] The extra-high level(4) is less common, being reserved for marking special emphasis or feeling or contrast.

EXERCISES

1. Read the following sentences aloud with the pitch patterns indicated:

   a) [2]That's [3]my car[1]
   b) The [2]operation lasted [2]ten [3]minutes[1]
   c) [2]One, [2]two, [2]three, [3]four[1]
   d) [3]One, [3]two, [3]three, [3]four[1]
   e) [3]One, [3]two, [3]three, [4]four[1]
   f) [2]What do you [3]want[1]
   g) [2]What do you [4]want[1]
   h) [2]What do [4]you [3]want[1]
   i) [2]George lost every single [1]game[3]
   j) [3]No, he [4]won the [3]last one[1]

2. Write out the following sentences and mark the pitch patterns as above:

   a) The guests departed.
   b) The waves smashed up the pier.
   c) Are you ready? No, are you?

d) Well, just look at those young hooligans!

e) (Telephone conversation)

> G: George Dougall here. Is that you, Ralph?
>
> R: Yes, Ralph speaking. What's the news?
>
> G: Only that Ethel has won the tennis singles championship.
>
> R: You're joking! Ethel? With that feeble backhand of hers? I can't believe it!
>
> G: You will! Actually, she's been practising hard this last month, and her backhand is nearly as good as her forehand now.

3. Example: He was little more than [2]a [3]*walking* [3]skeleton[1].

    He leant heavily on [2]a [3]*walking*[1]-stick[1].

Make up pairs of sentences illustrating similar contrasts of pitch, using the following words twice each:

a) drinking (e.g. water, cattle)

b) curling

c) dancing

d) running

e) melting

4. Each of the following sentences can – like C in the Sample – be read with different pitch patterns for different situations. Indicate the various possibilities.

a) What are you doing? (normal inquiry; panic; exasperation)

b) They went home yesterday.

c) Good morning, madam.

d) I've been here ten minutes.

e) Was that your father?

5. In writing, the following sentences are ambiguous. Read each of them aloud with two different speech

patterns. Then write each out twice and mark the important features of transition, stress, and pitch.

a) Alfred stood by his brother.
b) They passed by the narrow lane.
c) $x = 2 \times 4 + 3$.
d) They tore up the road.
e) Are you sure that one was open?
f) I found him drinking water.
g) The caretaker spoke to the children roughly at ten o'clock.
h) I sometimes wonder what good honest work is.
i) All the books on modern language teaching have been borrowed.
j) You shouldn't go out with anybody.

Part Two

SENTENCE PATTERNS

6 · Labels, Headings, and Messages

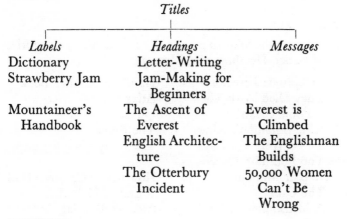

Labels	*Headings*	*Messages*
Dictionary	Letter-Writing	
Strawberry Jam	Jam-Making for Beginners	
Mountaineer's Handbook	The Ascent of Everest	Everest is Climbed
	English Architecture	The Englishman Builds
	The Otterbury Incident	50,000 Women Can't Be Wrong

COMMENT

A *Label* is a word or cluster indicating the nature of the thing (jam-pot, book, etc.) to which it is attached. A *Heading* is a word or cluster indicating what the headed material (book, article, newspaper report, etc.) is about. Labels and Headings are both responses to implied questions. The former in effect answers 'This is x' to the question 'What is it?'. The latter answers 'This is about x' to the question 'What is it about?'.

Messages differ in two important ways from both Labels and Headings. Though generally of more than one word, they do not form single clusters (Everest | is Climbed, The Englishman | Builds, etc.). Nor need they be taken as responses to questions; they tell something in their own right. 'Everest is Climbed' was the title of a book, but it might equally well have been a telegram bearing important news. On the other hand, 'The Ascent of Everest' does not positively state that the peak was reached; the same title might have done for a book about unsuccessful attempts on the mountain.

EXERCISES

1. Allocate the following book-titles to the three categories of Label, Heading, and Message:

Telephone Directory	Handy Reference Book
They Died With Their Boots Clean	Atlas
King Solomon's Ring	Quicker Reading
Those Were the Days	The Bible
The Fountain Overflows	The Lady's Not for Burning
Repair Manual	How Many Children Had Lady Macbeth?
The Gun	
A Midsummer Night's Dream	All's Well That Ends Well
The Kon-Tiki Expedition	Tales Out of School
England Made Me	Room at the Top
The Mountain is Young	

2. Find – among book-titles, magazine articles, newspaper reports, etc. – five more Labels, five Headings, and five Messages.

3. Sort out the following newspaper headlines, which are either Headings or Messages:

Moscow Mystery
Trailer Turns Over
Polio Vaccine Delays
One Vote Made Him Alderman
Experts Fail
Rain Ruins Roses
Children Flee as Home Collapses
Britain's First Atomic Injury Law Suit Claim
Russian Rocket Will Become Planet
Rights of Mental Patients
Lightning Causes Chaos
False Alarm
Prisoner Escapes
City One Way Traffic Problem Solution
Man Dies As He Fights Blaze

4. Invent ten newspaper headlines, five of them Headings,
   the other five Messages.
5. Can you think of five film-titles that are Messages (e.g.
   The Lady Is A Square)?

7 · Headings and Messages

SAMPLE

	Heading	*Message*
A]	Políce Search	Políce | seárch
	Peóple Like Maria	People líke | María
B]	Políce Search	Políce search | contínues
	Peóple Like Maria	Peóple like Maria|are ráre

COMMENT

A] Ambiguity is possible where, as in newspaper headlines, the little words that signal a Heading (e.g. *a* police search) or a Message (e.g. *the* police *are* searc*hing*) are left out. Similarly, the film-title 'People Like Maria' might mean either 'people resembling Maria' (Heading) or 'People *do* like Maria' (Message).

B] The first part of a Message is commonly itself a kind of Heading. It follows that it is normally possible so to add to a Heading as to build up a Message.

EXERCISES

1. Explain the ambiguity in the following, reading each aloud in the two possible ways:

    Giant Waves Down Funnel
    Girl Guides Bus
    Fresh Herrings Plan to Beat Slump
    National Health Service Ban Stays
    (Bus On Fire) Passengers Alight

2. Find or invent five more examples of this kind of ambiguity.

3. Turn the following Headings into Messages by adding to them or by making slight changes in the wording (e.g. Cabinet's Resignation/Cabinet Resigns):

    Cuban Revolt
    Moscow Mystery
    Steel Prices
    New City Centre Traffic Light System
    Colour Bar
    Olympic Games Television Broadcast Controversy
    Cup Final Postponement
    Gas Heater Explosion

Beauty Queen Competition
Orchestra's Final Rehearsal

4. Find or invent five more such Headings and turn them into Messages.

8 · Two-item Predications

SAMPLE

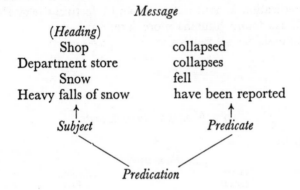

Message

(*Heading*)	
Shop	collapsed
Department store	collapses
Snow	fell
Heavy falls of snow	have been reported

Subject *Predicate*

Predication

COMMENT

We have already seen (in Section 7) that Headings are commonly word-clusters and that additions to them can produce Messages. The addition itself may be a single word or word-group. It never merges with the Heading to form a cluster; it is commonly separated in speech by a distinct juncture or pause.

In other words, if we use the term Item to include both word and cluster a Message normally comprises at least two items. Their grammatical names are Subject and Predicate, and together they make a Predication. Messages are distinguished from other sequences of words in that they predicate.

EXERCISES

1. Make a list of ten two-item predications, beginning with a two-word predication and progressively introducing clusters of increasing size.
2. Find ten two-item predications from newspaper headlines.
3. Write five short passages in each of which a two-word predication is used naturally and effectively (e.g. I've always found humans more interesting than animals. Animals are all much the same; *people vary*).

9 · *Nominal Headwords*

SAMPLE

	Predication	
	Subject Nominal	Predicate Verb
A]		
	Iron	rusts.
	Pig-*iron*	rusts.
	Unpainted *iron*	rusts.
	Iron of poor quality	rusts.
	Unpainted *iron* of poor quality	rusts.
	Iron that is neglected instead of being painted regularly	rusts.
B]	*It*	ought to be painted regularly.

COMMENT

A] The basic word in all Predicates is called a Verb; we shall look more closely at Verbs later. The basic word in the Subject may conveniently be called a *Nominal*. It may be a single word, or it may be the *Headword* of a cluster or set of clusters. The remainder of the cluster is an Adjunct or series of Adjuncts expanding the Headword.

B] Instead of repeating a Nominal word or word-group we often use a Pronominal such as 'it', 'he', 'she', 'they'.

EXERCISES

1. Using the above set of sentences as a model, expand the Subject item in each of the following predications in as varied a way as possible. Underline the Headword throughout.

   a) Flowers die.
   b) Acid burns.
   c) Rain fell.
   d) Father recovered.
   e) Bells pealed.

2. Find or invent five two-word predications and expand the Subject Nominals similarly.

3. Underline the Headword in the Subject of each of the following predications. Then, by reversing the process shown in the Sample above, reduce them stage by stage to two-word predications.

   a) The theatre box office opened.
   b) Leading Atomic Energy Authority Official Resigns.
   c) The patent lock on the door jammed.

c

d) A tall dark well-dressed man whom I thought I recognized entered.

e) All members of the local youth club committee with more than one year's service contributed.

4. In 'The *woman* with the heavy suitcase obviously feared *she* would miss the train' the Pronominal 'she' refers back to the Subject Nominal cluster based on the Headword 'woman'. Write three sentences to show how the Pronominals 'he', 'it', and 'they' may operate similarly.

10 · Verb Clusters

SAMPLE

Subject Nominal	Predication	Predicate Verb
Iron		*rusts.*
Iron		may *rust.*
Iron		ought not to *rust.*
Iron		might not have *rust*ed.
Iron		will go on *rust*ing.

COMMENT

The Predicate Verb, like the Subject Nominal, may be a single word or a cluster. A Verb Cluster, like a Nominal Cluster, consists of a basic Headword with additions. These additions may be word-endings (e.g. -ed, -ing) or other words or both. The Verb Cluster would not often consist of more than four or five words, but considerably larger expansions are possible, though cumbersome (e.g. I *don't want to be forced to begin to try to make* money).

EXERCISES

1. Expand the Verb item in each of the following predications to form clusters of several words each. Underline the Verb Headword throughout.
   a) Arsenal won.
   b) Everybody laughed.
   c) Those gates creak.
   d) The storm passed.
   e) The roof of the old barn leaks.

2. Expand both Nominal and Verb item in the following predications, underlining both Headwords throughout.
   a) Actors rehearse.
   b) Women screamed.
   c) Children ran.
   d) Bees swarm.
   e) Neighbours complained.

3. Write out the following sentences. Separate Subject and Predicate by a vertical line and underline the Subject and Verb Headwords.
   a) The six young athletes from the Soviet Union have arrived.
   b) The main force of the enemy seemed to be withdrawing.
   c) Among the younger women competitors several may not have been trying.
   d) Those who are not interested ought not to attend.
   e) The cargo in the ship's hold went on burning.
   f) Holders of complimentary tickets will not have to be kept waiting.
   g) People from all parts of the country were expected to attend.

h) Noisy, dirty, untidy children ought not to be admitted.

i) The rest of the evening's performance proceeded without interruption.

j) Of the many foreign people who come to live in Britain most settle down quickly.

11 · Phrasal Verbs

SAMPLE

A]   They *enter*.   They *come in*.

They *enter*ed.   They *came in*.

They were *enter*ing.   They were *coming in*.

They ought not to   They ought not to

have *enter*ed.   have *come in*.

B] Headword: enter   come in/came in/

com- in

Infinitive: to enter   to come in

to accompany   to go along with

to despise   to look down upon

COMMENT

A] The basic Verb in the left-hand column is 'enter'; the Verbs after the first one are elaborations of 'enter'. But the basic Verb in the right-hand column is not 'come' but 'come *in*'. To all intents and purposes 'come in' is as much a single Verb as 'enter'. (Speech intonation ties the two bits together: contrast 'They came ín' with 'They cáme | in a táxi'.) All such combinations of Verbs with small words (called Particles) such as 'in', 'out', 'of', 'up', 'down', 'to', 'with' can be treated as single units and may be called *Phrasal Verbs*.

B] With Verbs such as 'come' the headword has variant forms (come/came; swim/swam/swum). It is usual and convenient to refer to Verbs in terms of their Infinitive forms—(to) come, (to) go, etc.

EXERCISES

1. What is the Infinitive of the Verb in each of the following sentences? To what single-word Infinitive is each more or less equivalent?

   a) He got up from his chair.
   b) We put up with the inconveniences as long as possible.
   c) The lorry caught up with us at the traffic lights.
   d) All the children took after their mother rather than their father.
   e) She did not give in without a remarkable struggle.
   f) The organizers put off the festival to the next month.
   g) I never run across you these days.
   h) Though of very different dispostions, they never fell out.
   i) I managed to get out of going.
   j) The police were looking into the murder.

2. Complete the following lists by inserting the missing Verbs:

   to go up
                          to watch
                          to extract
   to get on with
   to do away with
                          to descend
   to look up to
                          to return
                          to extinguish
   to get away (e.g. from pursuer)

3. Substitute one-word Verbs for the Phrasal Verbs in the following sentences without changing the meaning more than necessary:

   a) I hope to look up my Scottish cousins when I go to Edinburgh.
   b) The secretary turned down the proposal.
   c) In most countries red stands for danger.
   d) They put off their wedding for a year.
   e) The thieves made off with a large safe.
   f) Both lifeboats turned over in the heavy seas.
   g) The enemy came on with flags flying.
   h) She unwittingly gave away the secret hiding-place.
   i) The whole school came together for morning prayers.
   j) Nobody came out of the house while I was there.

4. Explain the possible ambiguity in:

   a) What are you looking for?
   b) At last he came across the street.
   c) The detective was looking into the case.
   d) Our dog always goes for the evening paper.
   e) German Attacks Peter Out In Desert.

5. Find or invent five newspaper headlines containing Phrasal Verbs.

12 · Agreement of Number

SAMPLE

	Subject	Predicate
A]	Pigs	grunt.
	The pig	grunts.
	The pigs	*have* been grunting.
	Our pig	*does* grunt.

	Subject	*Predicate*
B]	The committee	is/are agreed.
	The committee	were quarrelling among themselves.
	None of us	has/have the right to criticize.
c]	Egg and bacon	makes a useful quick meal.
	Five minutes	*is* not long enough.
	Five miles	seems a considerable distance.

COMMENT

A] There are commonly variant forms of Nominal and Verb to indicate Number – Singular or Plural. Normally Subject Nominals and Verbs agree in Number – both Singular or both Plural.

B] Occasionally the Subject Nominal, though Singular in form, 'feels' more or less plural in sense. For instance, according to whether the committee seems to speak with one or many voices, it selects either the Singular or the Plural Verb.

c] On the other hand, some Subjects, though in form clearly Plural, are felt to be Singular (*one* meal, *one* period of time, *one* distance) and so select Singular Verbs.

EXERCISES

1. Which of the two Verb forms in the following seems to you either the only possible one or the preferable one? Why?

   a) The family was/were all present.
   b) The enemy seems/seem to be all around us.
   c) Bread and butter is/are just what we want.

d) The government has/have decided to introduce fresh legislation.

e) I found that pen and paper was/were what I missed most.

f) Parliament has/have not yet discussed the matter.

g) The jury was/were out of the courtroom for three hours.

h) The audience was/were expressing its/their feelings very decidedly.

i) The crowd is/are becoming impatient.

j) A mere handful of police was/were keeping the crowd back.

2. Write sentences in which the following items are used as Subject Nominals with Verbs that are in form distinctively Singular or Plural.

a) The public . . .

b) Many a woman . . .

c) Neither of the boxers . . .

d) None of the competitors . . .

e) The pitching and tossing of the boat . . .

13 · Three-item Predications

SAMPLE

	Subject Nominal	Predicate Verb
A]	Iron	rusts.
	Snow	has fallen.
	The judge	frowned.
	The postman's daughter	is going to sing.

	Subject	Predicate	
B]	*Nominal*	*Verb*	*3rd Item*
	Iron	is	*metal.*
	Snow	has ruined	the *harvest.*
	The judge	sentenced	the *prisoner.*
	The postman's daughter	became	a film *star.*

COMMENT

A] These sentences are simple two-item predications.

B] Here the same Nominals with different Verbs make predications of a kind – but an incomplete kind. A third item is needed to complete each. In other words, these are three-item predications. Notice that the third item may be a single word or a cluster – in the latter case based on the italicized headword.

EXERCISES

1. Write five pairs of sentences similar to the above, i.e. each pair comprising a two-item and a three-item predication using the same Subject.

2. Classify the following sentences as two-item or three-item patterns. Where an item is a cluster, indicate its headword.

    a) Sudden cramp attacked the swimmer's legs.

    b) The long spell of fine weather was breaking up.

    c) The main obstacle to progress was the attitude of the peasants.

    d) Violent disagreement ought to have been anticipated.

    e) The shop-assistant pulled down the blinds.

    f) The experiment proved a complete success.

    g) None of the organizers had expected such a vast audience.

h) He felt master of the situation.

i) The car's headlamps might not have been working properly.

j) Few child prodigies become expert adult performers.

3. Classify the following newspaper headlines in the same way.

a) The Army Will Look Different.

b) Provincial Press Closes Down.

c) Mikoyan Talks Raise Hopes and Doubts.

d) Overnight the Green Fence Became White.

e) Statement in Parliament is Expected.

f) Cup-tie Caused Bus Service Chaos.

g) U.S. Giant Satellite is a 'Talking Moon'.

h) Police Chief Hands In His Resignation.

i) Miner Is New Civic Chief.

j) Skilled Men Need Not Apply.

4. Find or invent five more two-item and five more three-item headlines.

14 · Subject Complements and Direct Objects

SAMPLE

A] Iron is a *metal*.   The judge sentenced the *prisoner*.
Men are *animals*.   Men hunt *animals*.
George made an ex-   George made a model *aeroplane*.
cellent *captain*.

x (is) x' x (affects) y
Subject + Verb +   Subject + Verb +
Subject Complement   Direct Object.

B] Father did not look   Father shot *himself.*
    himself.
C]   ?   Helen made an excellent model   ?
D] It's mé. It is Í.   I sáw him.

COMMENT

A] Rough sketches illustrating the left-hand sentences
might show just single 'things' – a bar of iron, an ape-
man, an efficient-looking George. If the Subject is
called x, then the third item is an aspect of x and may
be called x'. But sketches of the right-hand sentences
need two 'things' – judge and prisoner, huntsmen and
foxes, George and his plane. The third item here is
quite different from the Subject; it may be labelled y.
The usual grammatical names for x' and y are Subject
Complement and Direct Object.

B] The so-called reflexive construction is slightly excep-
tional, in that the Direct Object is the same 'thing' as
the Subject. It is reasonable, however, to argue that
Father was treating himself as he might have treated a
Direct Object such as a fox.

C] The characteristic Verb of the S + V + SC pattern is
a form of what is sometimes called an equational Verb –
'to be', 'to become', 'to seem', and the like – while the
Verb of the S + V + DO pattern is characteristically
a 'doing' or 'affecting' word. Since the Verb 'to make'
can be used either in a 'being' or in a 'doing' sense,
ambiguity is possible. Presumably, however, the context would make it clear whether Helen became a
mannequin or put together a small-scale reproduction.

(NOTE: A useful test for distinguishing the S + V + SC
from the S + V + DO construction is that the latter,
but not the former, can be transposed into the so-called

'passive' construction: e.g. Animals *are hunted* by men.
See Section 24 below, especially Exercise 3.)

D] There is often in speech a marked variation in the
distribution of stress in the two patterns, especially
when the Verb in the S + V + SC construction is part
of 'to be' and when the third item is a Pronominal.
Thus, in 'It is Í' and 'It's mé', the final Pronominal
takes major stress and the Verb is hardly pronounced,
let alone stressed. On the other hand, in 'I sáw him' the
Verb takes major stress and the Pronominal DO is reduced to an unstressed 'm sound.

EXERCISES

1. Pick out the headwords of the three basic items in each
of the following sentences and then classify the pattern
of each as S + V + SC or S + V + DO:

   a) The new prison governor looked every inch a soldier.
   b) Church bells often sound more attractive from a
   distance.
   c) The old fisherman used to tell hair-raising sea-stories.
   d) Young boys do not willingly wash themselves.
   e) Very few of the students could keep up with the
   lecturers.
   f) The retiring officers will remain honorary members
   of the club.
   g) Modern gramophones will play records of several
   different speeds.
   h) Some of the smaller rivers often ran completely
   dry.
   i) Fire interrupted the last performance.
   j) The retaining screw had somehow worked dangerously loose.

2. Classify the following newspaper headlines similarly to the above:

   a) Judge Stops Marriage.
   b) Rotodynes Would Need City Airports.
   c) Famous Film Star Turns Diplomat.
   d) Attacks Worry Dublin.
   e) Yacht Steers Itself.
   f) Diamond Discovery Was Rag Hoax.
   g) Russian Rocket Will Become Planet.
   h) Papers Continue Half-Size.
   i) Docile Pitch Ensures Tame Ending.
   j) This Is Probably My Last Wimbledon.

3. Classify similarly the three-item predications included in Exercises 2 and 3 of Section 13.

4. Find or invent ten headlines, five of the S + V + SC pattern, five of the S + V + DO pattern.

5. Sort the following sentences into three groups according to their basic patterns: i) S + V; ii) S + V + SC; iii) S + V + DO.

   a) The election was a fraud.
   b) Borrowers don't always return library books.
   c) He returned a national hero.
   d) My brother will have been champion three times.
   e) The telephone in his room kept on ringing.
   f) They lost themselves in the forest.
   g) The milk tasted distinctly sour.
   h) Hilarious celebrations were still going on.
   i) The smallest of the boats in the race turned right over.
   j) Parents ought to be stricter.

15 · Subject Complements

A	*B*
This play is *fun*.	This play is *funny*.
She became *secretary*.	She became *blind*.
This seems *the answer*.	This seems *correct*.

S + V + SC

Nominal + Verbal + Nominal

S + V + SC

Nominal + Verbal + ?

COMMENT

All the S + V + SC sentences we have so far examined have been of the A type, in which the SC headword is a Nominal, i.e. the sort of word that could also operate as a Subject headword (e.g. The *fun* lasted all night. The *answer* proved correct). But the Subject Complements under B are different. They are not the sort of words that normally cluster with a/an/the and have Plural forms (e.g. an answer, the secretaries). They are the sort of item we have seen clustering with a Nominal headword – e.g. this *funny* business, a *blind* man, the *correct* answer – and they have variants such as 'funnier', 'more correct', 'totally blind'. This kind of word, because it characteristically clusters with a Nominal or (as Subject Complement) links up with a preceding Nominal, may conveniently be called an *Adnominal*.

EXERCISES

1. Identify the S + V + SC pattern in each of the following sentences and state whether each SC or SC headword is Nominal or Adnominal:

  a) More rain is likely.
  b) The Russian rocket will become a minor planet.
  c) The cold war is getting hotter.
  d) The dog was standing guard over the grave.
  e) John remained master of the situation.
  f) Most of us were feeling thoroughly miserable.
  g) Our early arrival seemed a great surprise to him.
  h) The entire consignment of cheese had turned slightly sour.
  i) It tasted extremely unpleasant.
  j) The youngest of the gang turned informer.

2. Find or invent ten newspaper headlines containing Subject Complements, five Nominal, five Adnominal.

3. Example: The play was *a success*. (Nominal)
         The play was *successful*. (Adnominal)

Make up five more pairs of S + V + SC sentences in which the same S + V pair is followed first by a Nominal and then by an Adnominal of much the same meaning.

16 · Direct and Indirect Objects

SAMPLE

A] *Subject   Verb   Subject Complement*
  Helen   became ⎫
  Helen   made   ⎬ an excellent model (= mannequin)

B] *Subject*   *Verb*   *Direct Object*

   Alec   made   a large model (of a house)

   Helen (also) made   an excellent model (of a house)

C] *Subject*   *Verb*   *?*   *Direct Object*

   Helen   gave   Jane   her model (of a house)

   Helen   made   Jane   a model (of a house)

COMMENT

Pattern C is obviously nearer to B than to A. The 'model' (of a house) in C is as much a DO as in B. In fact, C is virtually B plus 'Jane'. 'Jane' is not another DO – she is not directly 'made' or 'given'. But she is affected by the making or giving. Such an item is normally called an *Indirect Object* (IO). Characteristically it comes between Verb and DO and follows Verbs such as 'give', 'send', 'bring', 'present', 'teach'. It is normally a Nominal or Pronominal and frequently denotes a living creature (since most giving, sending, etc. is done to people or animals).

EXERCISES

1. Identify the S + V + IO + DO pattern in the following sentences.

   a) The ship's steward eventually brought us morning coffee.

   b) Nobody could have done the visiting team a greater service.

   c) His persistent attempts to film Shakespeare's plays in the end cost him a small fortune.

   d) I owe my parents everything.

   e) Her unexpected arrival set the organizers an awkward problem.

f) The company promised its employees full compensation.

g) It serves you right.

h) Typing always gives me a severe headache.

i) I shall never forgive him his outrageous behaviour.

j) From time to time the trainer threw the animals lumps of sugar.

2. In which of the following newspaper headlines does the S + V + IO + DO pattern operate?

a) Mad Bulls Bother Farm Hands.

b) Premier Gives Railways Top Priority.

c) Four Horn Blasts Cost Him 10*s*.

d) Canadian Students Will Be Guests of City Shipowner.

e) War's Biggest Hoax Makes Exciting Film.

f) The Baby Sets the Duke a Problem.

g) Man Dies After Brawl in Street.

h) Britain Offers Cyprus 'Association'.

i) Boy Taught Men a Lesson.

j) Indonesia Gets Tough With China.

3. Find or invent five newspaper headlines based on the S + V + IO + DO pattern.

4. Add ten short sentences to the following example of the S + V + IO + DO pattern, using as many different Verbs as you can (e.g. tell, owe, ask, serve, cost):

   We sent him congratulations.

5. Example:

   | My uncle sold bicycles. | S + V + DO |
   | My uncle sold me a bicycle. | S + V + IO + DO |

Make up pairs of sentences similar to the above, using the Verbs 'bring', 'send', 'lend', 'sing', 'ask', 'play', 'drop', 'forgive', 'promise', 'write'.

D

6. Example:

You promised me a subscrip-tion.	S + V + IO + DO
You promised a subscription.	S + V + DO
You promised me.	S + V + IO

Make up trios of sentences similar to the above, based on the Verbs 'teach', 'owe', 'write', 'pay', 'forgive'.

7. Why is the following sentence ambiguous?

He took her presents.

17 · Object Complements

SAMPLE

A] 1. Helen became an excellent (artist's) model.   S + V + SC

2. Helen made an excellent (toy) model.   S + V + DO

3. Helen made Jane an excellent (toy) model.   S + V + IO + DO

B] 1. Experience made Helen an excellent (artist's) *model*.

2. I never thought him a *cheat*.

C] 1. Experience made her *confident*.   S + V + DO + ?

2. I never thought him *dishonest*.

COMMENT

A] These are the three patterns we have just examined, two with three basic items, one with four.

b] Sentence B.1 has (like A.3) four basic items and (like A.2) a DO. Nevertheless, it resembles A.1 even more closely; it means that experience caused Helen to become an excellent model. In fact, 'model' is in both cases a Complement linked with 'Helen'. Because in A.1 'Helen' is the Subject, 'model' is called the Subject Complement. In B.1, where 'Helen' is the DO, 'model' is called the *Object Complement*. An OC characteristically follows Verbs such as 'make' (in the sense of 'cause to be'), 'call', 'elect', 'think', 'consider'.

b, c] Like Subject Complements, Object Complements may be either Nominal (model, cheat) or Adnominal (confident, dishonest).

EXERCISES

1. Identify the S + V + DO + OC pattern in each of the following sentences. State whether each OC headword is Nominal or Adnominal in character.

 a) Roots and berries kept the travellers alive throughout their ordeal.
 b) The new cast made the play an enormous success.
 c) We must keep Britain tidy.
 d) His constant boasting in the end bored all the visitors stiff.
 e) Her passionate appeals left him quite indifferent.
 f) The class elected Rosemary form captain.
 g) They appointed George vice-captain.
 h) Children ought not to call each other liars.
 i) No one would make himself responsible for the outing.
 j) The decorators were going to paint all the woodwork bright green.

2. Which of the following newspaper headlines are based on the S + V + DO + OC pattern?

   a) Local Roof Slates Would Make Rents Higher.
   b) Tragedy Struck Homes of Nineteen Children.
   c) Bonn Army Is Ready for Worst.
   d) Smoking Set Bed Alight.
   e) Four Horn Blasts Cost Him Ten Shillings.
   f) Socialist Calls Test 'Useless'.
   g) Class Sets Teacher Problem.
   h) Police Think Missing Man Murderer's Victim.
   i) Rain Had the Last Word.
   j) Good Neighbours Kept Me Alive.

3. Find or invent five more newspaper headlines on the S + V + DO + OC pattern.

4. Comment on anything odd or interesting about the sentence:

   > She made him a good husband because she made him a good wife.

5. Add ten short sentences to the following examples of the S + V + DO + OC pattern, using as many different Verbs as you can (e.g. elect, turn, consider, prove):

Delays	made	him	furious.
Uncle Tom	found	golf	a fascinating game.

6. Example:

Helen became expert.	S + V + SC
Experience made Helen expert.	S + V + DO + OC

   Add to each of the following sentences the other sentence (with SC or OC) needed to make a pair corresponding to the example given:

   a) The lamplight turned his face yellow.
   b) A Persian cat remained her constant companion.
   c) The judges declared him the winner.

d) The plants grew strong.

e) We found the heat almost unbearable.

f) We all felt guilty.

g) Nobody thought him capable of such treachery.

h) John was the loser.

i) No amount of practice will make you a golfer.

j) The newspaper seemed thicker than usual.

7. Write five more pairs of sentences like those in the example in Exercise 6 above.

18 · Five Basic Patterns

SAMPLE

S	V	SC	IO	DO	OC
I. A] Tinned food	keeps.				
B] Tinned food	keeps	fresh.			
C] George	kept			rabbits.	
D] George	kept		us	seats.	
E] Blankets	kept			them	warm.
II. A] The thief	made off.				
B] He	was made	secretary.			
C] Mother	made			a cake.	
D] The tailor	made		him	a suit.	
E] The pitching	made			us	sea-sick.

COMMENT

Few verbs are flexible enough to be used in a natural way in all five major sentence patterns. In Group I, A is a little unlikely (though reasonable enough if slightly expanded to 'Tinned food keeps indefinitely'). If, as in Group II, we include for this purpose Phrasal Verbs (e.g. 'made off') and Passive forms (e.g. 'was made'), it is possible to make a few more complete sets.

EXERCISES

1. Using Phrasal Verbs and Passive forms when necessary, make up sets of sentences, similar to those in the Sample, based on the following Verbs:

   find, leave, call, get, stand.

2. Which of the five patterns (A–E) operates in each of the following sentences?

   a) The night-watchman had raised the alarm.
   b) A large furniture store was on fire.
   c) Several fire-engines raced by.
   d) The narrow streets allowed the firemen little space.
   e) The fierce heat made their work doubly difficult.
   f) Most newspapers set their readers crossword puzzles.
   g) These puzzles set the readers thinking.
   h) They have to use their intelligence.
   i) Some give up.
   j) The clues may seem unhelpful.

3. Compose a sequence of five sentences (as in Ex. 2 *a–e* or *f–j* above) about a single topic, using each of the five basic patterns.

4. Find or invent two newspaper headlines to illustrate each of the five basic patterns.

5. Though few Verbs can be used in all five patterns, many can be used in more than one: e.g. 'to drop' in:

The temperature *dropped*.	– A
The scrum half *dropped* the ball.	– C
I'll *drop* you a postcard.	– D

   Write sentences to show how the following verbs can be used in the patterns indicated.

to feel	– Patterns B, C.	
to shine	–	A, C.
to send	–	D, E.

to look	–	A, B, C.
to give (up)	–	A, D.
to grow	–	A, B, C, D.
to hold	–	A, B, C, E.
to drive	–	A, B, C, E.
to promise	–	A, C, D.
to teach	–	A, C, D.

6. Show how, in the absence of a fuller context, each of the following sentences is ambiguous and might fit either of two patterns:

   a) They found the old woman a help.

   b) She called him a horse.

   c) The Smiths are always entertaining.

   d) Indian Braves Fire.

   e) GET YOUNGER EVERY DAY. (Advertisement for beer)

7. Explain how, in spite of apparent similarities, the following pairs are based on different patterns:

   a) Her best friend gave her money.
   Her best friend stole her money.

   b) The strongest of the men made himself leader.
   The strongest of the men made himself a boat.

   c) Boys Feared Drowned.
   Boys Feared Ghosts.

   d) His brother kept him warm.
   His brother kept him a seat.

   e) He returned a changed man.
   He returned his library book.

   f) It worked loose.
   It worked loosely.

   g) Jordan Sets Briton Free.
   Jordan Sets Britain Problem.

   h) The nurse took her away.
   The nurse took her temperature.

i) He felt nothing.
   He felt exhausted.
j) She found her cousin a flat.
   She found her cousin a bore.

8. It is sometimes possible to use either the S + V + IO + DO or the S + V + DO + OC pattern to convey much the same sense as may be expressed in the simpler S + V + DO pattern. Thus:

i)   S   V   DO
   The keepers   fed   the animals.
        S   V   IO   DO
   The keepers   gave   the animals   food.

ii)   S   V   DO
   Men   have tamed   many animals.
        S   V   DO   OC
   Men   have made   many animals   tame.

Make up a sentence based on either the IO or the OC four-item pattern to correspond in meaning to each of the following. In each case underline and label the IO or OC.

a) They rewarded us.
b) The Church canonized Joan of Arc.
c) The journey tired him.
d) Nobody answered the policeman.
e) His wounded leg troubled him.
f) The gamekeeper thrashed the two boys.
g) Nobody can simplify Einstein's theory.
h) The excessive publicity embarrassed him.
i) He always over-tipped the waiters.
j) Her explanation clarified the situation.

19 · Verbids

A]

S	V	DO		*Verbids*
He	anticipated	failure.	(S + V + Nominal)	
He	anticipated	*failing*.		-ing
He	expected	*to fail*.		Infinitive

B]

S	V	SC		
		criticism.	(S + V + Nominal)	
A critic's job	is	*criticizing*.		-ing
		to criticize.		Infinitive

C]

S	V	DO	DO	
The police	let	her	*go*.	
They	made	him	*stay*.	Infinitives
They	wanted	him	*to confess*.	

D]

S	V	DO	OC/DO		
Necessity	made	him	an inventor.	(OC Nominal)	
Necessity	started	him	*inventing*.	(OC or DO)	-ing
Necessity	made	him	*invent*.	(DO)	Infinitive

COMMENT

A] Two versatile forms of the Verb, the -ing form and the Infinitive with or without 'to', include among their many functions that of operating as Nominals. Let us for convenience call these two forms *Verbids*. (The traditional label – non-finite parts of the Verb – is rather clumsy.)

B] Verbids can be equivalent to Nominals used as Direct Objects (as in A), as Subject Complements (as in B), or as Subjects (e.g. by reversing the B sentences: 'Criticizing/To criticize is a critic's job').

C] In this common construction the Infinitive Verbid is

probably better considered as a second Direct Object than as an Object Complement. (This S + V + DO + DO pattern could be added to the list of five in Section 18.)

D] Here the Nominal fourth item in the first sentence is an Object Complement. The Infinitive in the third sentence, like 'confess' under C, is more like a Direct Object than anything else. The -ing Verbid in the second sentence is a border-line case between the two.

EXERCISES

1. Identify the basic pattern in each of the following headlines:

   a) City Council Wants Works Manager to Resign.
   b) Latin States Make U.S. Change Step.
   c) Dr Banda Refuses to be Freed.
   d) Civil Servants Prefer Waiting.
   e) Dentist Keeps Councillor Waiting.
   f) Government's Intention is to Resign.
   g) Minister Regrets Making Promises.
   h) Shopkeeper Lets Customers Help Themselves.
   i) Britain's Strongest Sport is Swimming.
   j) Assassins Make Franco Change His Mind.

2. Find or invent five more headlines using Verbids.
3. Use the two Verbid forms of each of the following Verbs in sentences based on two of the patterns in the Sample (i.e. as DO, SC, 2nd DO or OC):
   smile, laugh, work, fish, return.

20 · *Markers*

SAMPLE

I. A] Bees sting. S+V N+V
   B] i) Beetles are insects. ⎱ S+V+SC ⎧ N+V+N
       ii) Beetles are unpleasant. ⎰ ⎩ N+V+ADN
   C] Caterpillars ruin cabbages. S+V+DO N+V+N
   D] Farmers give pigs acorns. S+V+IO+DO N+V+N+N
   E] i) War makes men brutes. ⎱ S+V+DO+OC ⎧ N+V+N+N
       ii) War makes men brutal. ⎰ ⎩ N+V+N+ADN

II. A] Plovak*s* wibble. *The* plovak wibble*s*. *The* plovak*s* *are* wibbl*ing*.
    B] i) Plovak*s* *are* durfew*s*. *This* plovak *is* *a* durfew.
        ii) Plovak*s* *are* rolag. *All* plovak*s* *seem to be* rolag.
    C] Plovak*s* wibble durfew*s*. *Many a* plovak *has* wibbl*ed* *a* durfew.
    D] Bluskin*s* *give* wibble*s* durfew*s*.
    E] i) Chenk make*s* bluskin*s* wibble*s*.
        ii) Chenk make*s* bluskin*s* rolag.

COMMENT

Identifying a sentence pattern involves recognizing the number, order, and type of basic items. Because isolated Nominals, Verbs, and Adnominals are by no means always identifiable as such, because several patterns have the same number of items, and because these items may be of the same type (N + V + N in B (i) and C; N + V + N + N in D and E (i)) further clues are sometimes necessary and always useful. Such clues – let us call them *Markers* – become obvious when, as in II above, nonsense-words are used wherever possible.

There are many Markers besides those italicized above, but these represent the most important kinds.

Nominals characteristically have forms with and without -s, and may be preceded by Markers such as a, an, the, this, that, all.

Verbs indicating present time also have forms with and without -s. A Subject Nominal with -s normally operates with a Verb without -s, and vice versa (see Section 12 above – Agreement of Number). Most Verbs have forms in -ing or -ed and may be compounded with parts of 'to be', 'to have', or 'to do', or with 'may', 'might', 'ought', etc.

Certain patterns are marked by special Verbs. The Verb in S + V + SC is an equational Verb such as part of 'to be', 'to seem', 'to become', etc. The Verb in S + V + IO + DO is characteristically 'give' or its equivalent (send, present, etc.). The Verb in S + V + DO + OC is typically 'make' in the sense of 'cause to be', 'cause to become'.

Adnominals do not in English have separate Singular and Plural forms. (Bluskins are *rolag*. A bluskin is *rolag*.) But very many of them have variants of comparison. The markers for this are either 'more'/'most' or 'less'/'least' before the basic form or the suffix -er or -est. (The bluskins are *more rolag* than usual. The gorbl*est* bluskin is *less rolag* than a stirk.)

EXERCISES

1. Identify the pattern of each of the following and write a sensible sentence on the same pattern, keeping everything except the nonsense words:

   a) The tagron plegged our bodak.
   b) Many of the glospets were druffing.
   c) Floms are the cruvest tiggles.
   d) A slookin threw the scrib a flisper.
   e) The wesp appeared to grow morger and morger.
   f) Our blesh corvits made the trisp plunkey.
   g) An ost nackon taught the yubs vistok.

h) The sprags seemed storp.

i) The grumpit made my croler a hankle.

j) Few partils dreg.

2. Using some or all of the following basic forms, with suitable markers, write ten varied sentences. Each sentence should clearly belong to one of the basic patterns, and each pattern should be represented at least once.

Nominals:	crip, tulap, flentomit
Verbs:	solk, gimble, drale
Adnominals:	spig, cruvy, rosterpol

21 · Orders and Requests

SAMPLE

A] Stop!   (S) + V

Keep quiet.   (S) + V + SC

Hold this.   (S) + V + DO

Give me that.   (S) + V + IO + DO

Make yourself comfortable.   (S) + V + DO + OC

B] *Watch Stops.

*Plan Changes.

*Guard Plans Carefully.

*Ban Stays.

*Bury Smallpox Suspect.

[* Here, as elsewhere, 'bad' samples are marked with a warning asterisk.]

COMMENT

A] Sometimes, for emphasis or contrast, we begin an order or request with 'you' (*You* keep quiet! *You* make yourself comfortable, while I . . .). But more commonly the 'you' is taken for granted without actually being mentioned.

B] When normal markers (e.g. *The* watch stops/Watch *the* stops) are left out, as they often are in telegraphic and headline English, uncertainty whether an initial 'you' is intended can cause ambiguity.

EXERCISES

1. Copy out the following items and against each indicate its basic pattern, as in Sample A above:

a) Forgive us our trespasses.
b) Take care.
c) Don't look back.
d) Make it snappy!
e) Be a man!
f) Stand easy!
g) Keep Britain Tidy.
h) Ask me another!
i) Carry on!
j) Change places.

2. Find or invent five headlines or telegrams similarly ambiguous to those in Sample B above.

22 · *Markers – Ambiguity*

SAMPLE

*Navy Demands Change.
    ? S + V   = Nava*l* demands/have changed
or
    ? S + V + DO = Navy/demands/*a* change

*Official Reports Increased Production.

   ? S + V + DO = Official reports/*have* increased/
or   production
   ? S + V + DO = *An* official/has reported/increased
                              production

*Police Help Prostrate Victims.

   ? S + V + DO = Police/help/prostrat*ed* victims
or
   ? S + V + DO = Police/help *to* prostrate/victims

*Australians Set To Work.

   ? S + V   = Australians *have* started work
or
   ? S + V   = Australians *have been* set to work.

COMMENT

The omission of Markers like a/the (for Nominals) and to/
has/have been (for Verbs) can obscure the distinction not
only between the request-pattern and the statement-
pattern (see Section 21, Sample B), but, as shown above,
between and within statement-patterns.

EXERCISES

1. Explain the possible ambiguity in each of the following
   and show how the alternative meanings might have
   been distinguished by the use of Markers:

   a) Direct Traffic
   b) Dog Starved
   c) Baby Swallows Fly
   d) Pay Increases
   e) Demonstrators Fired On

2. The following headlines are possibly ambiguous, though
   one of the meanings is highly improbable. What are the
   two possibilities in each case?

a) Mother Charged Over Baby in Bath
b) New Student Riots in Turkey
c) Fish Strike Looms
d) Fish Talks at Grimsby
e) Motorist Refused a Licence

23 · Ellipsis

SAMPLE

A] Dog Starved
Bradman Bowled
Drain Sinks
B] Do you think this will do?
Do you think one will do?
C] *Do you think that one will do?

COMMENT

A] We have already seen how the omission of markers can cause ambiguity. (Did Bradman bowl? or was he bowled out? Is the drain sinking? or are we to drain the sink?)
B] The omission of a word that can safely be taken for granted – e.g. 'that' in these two sentences – is known as *Ellipsis*.
C] Ellipsis has to be managed carefully. This sentence needs re-writing either as 'Do you think one will do?' or as 'Do you think *that* that one will do?'

EXERCISES

1. Re-write the following elliptical newspaper headlines with the omitted words reinstated. Then state the basic pattern of each.

a) Rain Likely
b) Man Hit by Bottle Dies of Injury
c) Boys Feared Drowned
d) Stolen Car in Crash
e) Film Treat for the Orphans
f) Robbery Hearing Today
g) Children Stole Coal, Fined
h) £71 H.P. a Month, Court Told
i) No Significant Increase in Crimes of Violence
j) Woman Dead after House Explosion

2. Example: Explorer Found Guilty

Explorer Found Treasure

Make similar pairs to the above, using the following Verbs:

feared, believed, made, held, sent

Explain how ellipsis has made one of each pair apparently resemble the other in structure.

3. Ellipsis is very common in idiomatic expressions, e.g. (I) thank you. What words are taken for granted in the following familiar utterances?

No wonder.
Well I never!
What about supper?
Practice makes perfect.
(Shall we have a swim?) Yes, let's.

4. Ellipsis has made the following ambiguous. Explain the two meanings possible in each case.

a) Newcastle is nearer to Durham than Hexham.
b) Heart Stopped for Fifty Minutes.
c) Prisoner Refused Bail.
d) Fashion a Little Conservative.
e) Trainer Turned Down Flat.

E

24 · Passive Verbs

	Active				Passive		
S	V	DO			S	V	
They announced the results.					The results were announced.		
S	V	DO	OC		S	V	SC
They made the results public.					The results were made public.		
S	V	IO	DO		S	V	IO
They gave the candidates the results.					The results were given them.		
					S	V	DO
					The candidates were given the results		

COMMENT

One of the commonest markers is 'to be', used to distinguish the so-called Passive form of a Verb from its Active form. In most Active constructions the action denoted by the Verb is performed by the agent denoted by the Subject. If the agent is not known – e.g. in an unsolved murder case – a Passive construction enables us to say that 'The victim *was murdered*' without naming the murderer. Similarly, when the agent is comparatively unimportant – as in the examples above – a Passive construction allows the subject-position to be occupied by the more important other items – e.g. *the results* were announced/*the candidates* were given the results.

Where, as in the third Active sample, there are two Objects in the Active construction, two corresponding Passive constructions are possible – S + V + IO and S + V + DO. Logically, the former of these would seem the more reasonable; after all, it was the results, not the candidates, that were given. But Active constructions predominate in English; among them the S + V + DO pattern is extremely common and the S + V + IO (without DO) pattern very rare. Consequently, familiarity makes us favour the S + V + DO arrangement in the Passive construction, in spite of its illogicality. Furthermore, we tend to change the Passive S + V + IO construction by substituting a to-phrase for the IO – e.g. 'The results were given *to* the candidates.' (This substitution is not so common when the IO is a Pronominal. The answer to 'Where did you get that book?' may as readily be 'It was given *me*' as 'I was given it'.)

EXERCISES

1. Write sentences corresponding in meaning to the following, but using Passive instead of Active form, or vice versa.

   a) They made him vice-captain.
   b) The judges awarded her a consolation prize.
   c) The hall-porter has been murdered.
   d) Some-one had strangled him.
   e) The winner will be given a cheque.
   f) The missing car was found abandoned near the cliff.
   g) A receipt will be sent you in due course.
   h) We shall need a large number of envelopes.
   i) It turned the liquid dark green.
   j) They served us a magnificent lunch.

2. 'X was given Y' might mean either that 'X received Y' or that 'X was given to Y'. Context and sense normally select one or the other meaning. Occasionally, however, real ambiguity is possible. Which of the following sentences are ambiguous, and why? What prevents the others from being ambiguous?

   a) The offender was given a second chance.
   b) The wrong overcoat was given George.

c) The cheque was given the prize-winner.

d) (The animals in the zoo were sorted into pairs.) The lion was given the leopard as companion.

e) (The M.C. arranged pairs of dancing-partners.) Joan was given Henry; Mary was given Alec.

3. The pattern Nominal – Verb – Nominal might be either S + V + DO or S + V + SC. Usually the character of the Verb decides which. But some Verbs fit both patterns. In such cases the DO pattern can be detected by turning it round into the equivalent Passive construction. The SC pattern cannot be so reversed. Use this test to establish the pattern of each of the following:

a) She felt the mattress.

b) She felt mistress of the situation.

c) He finished deputy director of the firm.

d) He finished his work early.

e) The expedition proved a nightmare.

f) The expedition proved their theory.

g) The bell sounded the alarm.

h) The result sounded a certainty.

i) The play continued an enormous success.

j) The play continued its long run.

Part Three

WORD-ORDER

---

25 · *Variation of S + V Order*

		V	S	
A]		Came	the dawn.	
	Up	spake	brave Horatius.	
	Down	came	the rain.	
	Into the ring	leapt	the boxer's wife.	
	Next	followed	a cartoon film.	
	Tomorrow	will be celebrated	Trafalgar Day.	
B]	Here/There	are	the others.	
	There	were	few survivors.	
	There	was	no one	there.
C]	Where	was	Jack?	
		Did	you?	

		v	S	V
D]		Were	they	singing?
	How	do	you	do?
	When	will	the strike	end?

COMMENT

A] The order of the items in a basic pattern is always important and sometimes crucial. In extreme cases the reversal of the S + V order in a two-item predication would completely change the meaning. For example,

the unlikely 'Train flies' would become the equally unlikely but very different 'Flies train'.

Reversal is, however, possible and effective in certain circumstances. In the first three of these sentences
it is used for poetic or dramatic effect. In the other
sentences it follows time or place items, reducing the
emphasis on the centrally placed Verb and adding
force to the final Subject.

B] The neutral term here/there and the comparatively in-
significant central Verb leave all the weight for the final
Subject. Notice that, as the last sentence shows, the
initial here/there is a function-word (it is sometimes
called an expletive or 'filler'); it has not the sense of 'in
this/that place' carried by the full-word 'here/there'.
There is also a stress distinction; the full-word 'there'
carries a stronger stress than the expletive 'there',
which, moreover, is often 'reduced' in pronunciation to
a sound like 'ther'.

C] Reversal is normal in information-questions beginning
with 'where?', 'when?', 'how?', etc. It is only one of
several alternatives in Yes/No questions (i.e. questions
inviting confirmation or denial). The other alternatives
are the plain statement-order S + V with rising intonation in speech or a question-mark in writing (You
did? ↗) and the combination of statement order with
question-tag (You did, did you?).

D] When in questions the Verb contains more than one
part, the Subject usually splits it, making a partial reversal of the statement order. The Verbal meaning is
carried mainly in the second part; we therefore keep
the capital 'V' for that part. The first part, known
traditionally as an auxiliary Verb, may then be denoted
by a small 'v'.

EXERCISES

1. Identify the basic Subject and Verb items in the following sentences and state in which the standard S + V order is reversed:

   a) Near the door lay a bloodstained carpet.
   b) The revolver was still smoking.
   c) 'Here is the cause of all the trouble!'
   d) Into the valley of Death
      Rode the six hundred.
   e) The next day several women were arrested.
   f) His temperature rose rapidly.
   g) There died that day more than ten thousand people.
   h) Over there in the corner of the window is the very thing we want.
   i) The blood-red sun slowly sank behind the mountains.
   j) Here endeth the lesson.

2. Make up sentences to show how V + S reversals can follow each of these: never, never again, not always, upstairs, over there.

3. Make up five more sentences on the V + S pattern, using different time and place items from those in Exercise 2.

4. Identify the instances of full or partial reversal of the standard statement order in the following questions:

   a) Will he be coming along later?
   b) Your father actually apologized?
   c) Where was I?
   d) It fell apart in your hands, did it?
   e) Went the day well?
   f) Your sister is not going to come after all?

g) Ought not the senior vice-president of the club to attend?

h) Why did the car swerve violently to the right?

i) Shall we?

j) You were going to explain your late arrival, weren't you?

26 · Variation of S + V + SC Order

SAMPLE

	S	+	V	+	SC
A]	The postman's daughter-in-law		became		a film-star.
	The film-star		became		a postman's daughter-in-law.

	S + V + SC		V + S + SC
B]	He is not often so unreasonable.		Not often is he so unreasonable.

	SC + V + S
The performing seals were most remarkable.	Most remarkable were the performing seals.
It seemed very strange.	SC + S + V Very strange it seemed.

	S + V + SC		V + S + SC
C]	We are ready?		Are we ready?
	George was a goalkeeper?		Was George a goalkeeper?

	$\overline{\text{v} + \text{S} + \text{V}} + \text{SC}$
It would have been wrong?	Would it have been wrong?
It is difficult.	SC + V + S How difficult is it?

	SC + S + V
D] It is difficult.	How difficult it is!
It would be a nuisance.	What a nuisance it would be!

COMMENT

A] Variation of order in a S + V + SC pattern in which both S and SC are Nominals is rarely to be expected. Why?

B] Where the SC is an Adnominal, several variations are possible, giving varying distributions of emphasis.

c] As with the S + V pattern, questions can be framed with full or partial reversal of Subject and Verb.

D] For exclamations the most typical variation brings the SC in front of the S + V.

EXERCISES

1. In which of the following sentences is the standard S + V + SC order varied? How and to what effect?

a) United we stand; divided we fall.

b) The threat of a general strike loomed large.

c) Especially welcome was the possibility of a hot bath.

d) All day long the shop stayed shut.

e) Sweet are the uses of adversity.

f) Never again was I so foolhardy.

g) Before she could boil it the milk turned sour.

h) At no other time were the streets so crowded.

i) Throughout the castle every room felt damp.

j) Keener and keener the competition became.

2. What is the basic sentence pattern of each of the following? How and why does it vary from the standard statement pattern?

a) What a success this conference has been!

b) Was the conference successful?

c) Is the new engine proving economical?

d) How important is next week's examination?

e) What a lucky escape it seemed to have been!

f) Did you feel master of the situation?

g) Is mathematics a difficult subject?

h) How much more interesting the lecture could have been!

i) How much bigger than this was your garden?

j) How late is the train going to be?

3. What variations of standard item-order can you detect in the following sentences from the beginning of Edgar Allan Poe's story, 'The Black Cat'?

> 'For the narrative which I am about to pen, I neither expect nor solicit belief. Mad indeed would I be to expect it. . . . Yet, mad I am not – and very surely do I not dream.'

27 · Variation of S + V + DO Order

SAMPLE

S + V + DO	V + S + DO
A] One seldom has such an opportunity.	Seldom has one such an opportunity.

	DO + V + S
B] Dogs hate cats.	
The referee said 'No'.	'No', said the referee.

	DO + S + V
C] Mr Micawber has talent;	'Talent, Mr Micawber has;
Mr Micawber hasn't capital.	capital, Mr Micawber hasn't.'
He hated such people.	Such people he hated.

V + S + DO	v + S + V + DO
D] Have we time?	Does he take exercise?

DO + V + S	DO + v + S + V
What chance have we?	What can he be doing?

COMMENT

The S + V + DO pattern is very common indeed. We have noticed (in Section 24 above) how, in using a Passive Verb, the S + V + DO 'feel' tends to make us prefer 'The candidates were given the results' to the more logical 'The results were given the candidates'. We may see the same pressure in favour of 'It is me/us' (with the characteristic Object forms 'me/us' in the Object position) rather than 'It is I/we'. So strong is our sense of S + V + DO order that variations from it are comparatively few and somewhat special in character.

A] The right-hand sentence exemplifies the familiar reversal of Subject and Verb after a time-item ('seldom').

B] Complete reversal to DO + V + S is not normally to be expected. (Why?) But where the DO is clearly identified by speech-marks (or speech-intonation), reversal is possible and indeed common.

C] The variations here direct special emphasis to the initially placed DOs, pointing the contrast between them.

D] In questions full or partial reversal of Subject and Verb is again common. Direct Objects consisting wholly or partly of question-words such as 'what?', 'which?', 'whom?', 'whose?' normally come first.

EXERCISES

1. What variation of the standard S + V + DO order is made in each of the following sentences? And to what effect?

   a) 'Bend over!' ordered the headmaster.
   b) The gramophone he took away; but the piano he left behind.

c) In no circumstances have you the right to leave early.

d) Have you any small change?

e) Were you looking for me?

f) A horrible mess you've made of it!

g) Which camera shall we use?

h) He could stand most kinds of torture, but the tickling of his feet he could not endure for a second.

i) Whom did he accuse?

j) What alternative had she?

2. Make up a set of sentences equivalent in pattern to those given in the Sample above.

3. Explain the ambiguity of each of the following:

a) And all the air a solemn stillness holds.

b)   In a trice the wretched man
    The closing gate squeezed flat.

c) Odin the Dog of Darkness spied.

d) Then mocked the King his henchman,
    And spurned him from the gate.

e) And thus the son the fervent sire addressed.

4. Explain how sense of item-order in the S + V + DO pattern makes the following clear in spite of unusual features:

a) "er left I without a word.'

b) 'Us followed they all the way home.'

c) 'Him chased we down the street.'

28 · *Variation of S + V + IO + DO Order*

SAMPLE

	S + V + IO + DO	IO + S + V + DO
A]	He gave Joan nothing, but he gave George 10*s*.	Joan he gave nothing, but George he gave 10*s*.

B]   The manager gave him it.

S + V + DO + IO
The manager gave it him.

v + S + V + IO + DO
C] They wrote you an apology?   Did they write you an apology?

IO + v + S + V + DO
Who teaches you French?   Whom does he teach French?

DO + v + S + V + IO
Your father has given your mother   What has your father given your
a present?   mother?

COMMENT

A] A familiar kind of variation can bring the Indirect
Object to the prominent first position for the sake of
emphasis.

B] Pronominal Direct and Indirect Objects are less tied
to fixed positions than Nominals.

C] In questions the standard order can be used, with a
question-intonation or question-mark, and possibly
with a question-word (e.g. who?) as well. Partial reversal by 'splitting' the Verb is common. A question-
word Object (Direct or Indirect) usually takes first
position in the sentence.

EXERCISES

1. Make up a further set of sentences on the lines of the
Sample.

2. What variation of the normal S + V + IO + DO
pattern occurs in each of the following? To what
effect?

   a) I sent it you several days ago.

   b) How much money did he leave his wife?

   c) The girls they interviewed, but the boys they set
   written tests.

d) Has he forgiven you your rudeness?
e) Whom did you send a Christmas card?
f) Her youngest son she bought an electric train.
g) What did she buy her niece?
h) The steward brought it them almost immediately.
i) Which competitors did they award prizes?
j) Shall we play our guests that new record?

3. Write a paragraph in which at least two of these pattern-variations occur naturally and effectively.

29 · *Variation of S + V + DO + OC Order*

SAMPLE

S + V + DO + OC
A] They called their first son John.

DO + S + V + OC
Their first son they called John.

OC + S + V + DO
(I knew you were careless, but) dishonest I never thought you.

B] Who made him secretary?
They made him secretary?

v + S + V + DO + OC
Does the cold make your rheumatism worse?

DO + v + S + V + OC
Which room have you found most convenient?

COMMENT

A] As with other statement patterns, it is possible to re-distribute emphasis by changes in item-order. In these cases the Direct Object and the Object Complement gain prominence by being brought to the beginning of their predications.

B] The normal statement order, with question intonation or a question-word (e.g. who?), can be used for questions. The 'split' verb (especially with 'do') is very common, and the DO occurs first when it consists wholly or partly of a question-word.

EXERCISES

1. In which of the following sentences is the standard S + V + DO + OC pattern varied? What is the force of each variation?

   a) The President praised the loyalists; but the rebels he declared traitors.
   b) Whom do you think most reliable?
   c) The prisoner's answers were not making his case any stronger.
   d) I normally like fried food, but this fish I consider quite uneatable.
   e) Did your father find your explanation reasonable?
   f) Tactless she may be, but ungrateful you should not think her.
   g) No self-respecting parents will leave young children alone in the house.
   h) Which of the subjects are you finding most difficult?
   i) Are not many car-drivers making our roads death-traps?
   j) The dramatic society elected the oldest member president for the coming year.

2. Write a short paragraph in which a sentence based on the pattern DO + S + V + OC occurs naturally and effectively.

3. Write five questions, one of each of the five basic patterns, all illustrating full or partial reversal of Subject and Verb.

30 · Object Complements and Phrasal Verbs

A]
S + V + DO + OC

Constant use *made* the surface *smooth*.
Constant use *wore* the surface *smooth*.
The lamplight *turned* his face *green*.

The lamplight *turned* it *green*.
The lamplight *turned* everything within its range a brilliant *green*.
The lamplight *turned green* everything within its range.

B]
S + *Phrasal Verb* + DO

Constant use *wore away* the surface.
Constant use *wore* the surface *away*.
I *turned out* the light.
I *turned* the light *out*.
I *turned* it *out*.
The fire *burnt* everything *up* within its range.
The fire *burnt up* everything within its range.

COMMENT

The distinction between these two constructions is often very fine. Clues that may help are:

1. The Object Complement (e.g. smooth, green) is often clearly Adnominal, whereas the second part of the Phrasal Verb (e.g. away, out, up) is usually recognizable as a Particle.
2. The Phrasal Verb is equivalent to a single Verb (wore away = eroded; turned out = extinguished; burnt up = consumed). Not so the V + OC items under A; there is no Verb 'to greenify'. (There is a Verb 'to smooth', but it conveys a different sense.)
3. In Phrasal Verb constructions the Direct Object may or may not 'split' the Verb unit; often both alternatives are freely available, though a Pronominal DO cannot normally follow the Particle. In the OC construction the

DO nearly always separates Verb from OC; the exception is that a sizeable DO (e.g. 'everything within its range') may follow rather than precede the OC.

EXERCISES

1. Which of the two patterns operates in the following sentences?

   a) He painted his garden shed bright crimson.
   b) The accident held up the traffic for hours.
   c) The fog held it up still longer.
   d) He believes unfair any decision that doesn't favour him.
   e) She wrote the answers down.
   f) Neglect and decay were making the house unsafe.
   g) They found most bewildering their host's habit of suddenly disappearing.
   h) Nobody found out the cause of his strange behaviour.
   i) The weather turned most unpleasant.
   j) The small boat turned over at the height of the gale.

2. In the Sample the same basic Verb with two different additions (wore smooth/wore away; turned green/turned out) is used in a pair of sentences, one of S + V + DO + OC, the other of S + Phrasal V + DO pattern. Write similar pairs of sentences, using each of the following as the basic Verb:

   made, left, sets, kept, calls.

F

31 · *Proximity*

A] *The accused was sentenced to death for murdering an old lady *at Winchester Assizes*.

*The accused was sentenced to death *at Winchester Assizes* for murdering an old lady.

The accused was *at Winchester Assizes* sentenced to death for murdering an old lady.

At Winchester Assizes the accused was sentenced to death for murdering an old lady.

B] Some people *quickly* learn to type.

Some people learn to type *quickly*.

C] I *sincerely* wish to apologize.

I wish to apologize *sincerely*.

*I wish *sincerely* to apologize.

COMMENT

A] For a brief moment the reader of the first sentence wonders if the murder took place in court. He hesitates slightly over the second sentence, wondering if the death penalty is to be exacted in court. Dismissing both possibilities as unlikely, he assumes that it was the passing of the sentence that occurred in court, as clearly indicated in the other two versions.

B] The placing of 'quickly' in proximity either to 'learn' or to 'type' gives two quite different senses.

C] The placing of 'sincerely' in the first two sentences reflects a slight difference of meaning. In the third sentence 'sincerely' is placed ambiguously; it 'squints', looking both backward to 'wish' and forward to 'apologize'. In speech a terminal before or after 'sincerely' would distinguish between 'sincerely to apologize' and 'wish sincerely'. (An old prejudice against the 'split infinitive' discourages the perfectly clear 'to quickly type' or 'to sincerely apologize'.)

EXERCISES

1. In each of the following sentences there is a word or cluster which could occupy another position, thereby changing the meaning. Write out the alternative sentences (in some cases more than one variant is possible) and explain the change in meaning.

a) Children only are admitted on Saturdays.
b) Please copy out the notes you have written on foolscap.
c) Nobody wanted to dance with the elderly head-master's daughter.
d) The parish raised a further £100 towards the large sum required to restore the damage done by the death-watch beetle at a successful garden fête on June 23rd.
e) You can almost see it dying.
f) He himself began to paint.
g) They found the deserted village.
h) Happily she was married.
i) They made themselves generally objectionable.
j) He expressed his thanks naturally.

2. Write pairs of sentences to illustrate the different meanings made possible by the different placing of the following items:

nearly	pretty	only	practically	often
last Thursday		at least	with a stick	
after the match		as soon as possible		

3. Identify the 'squinting' item in each of the following. Write pairs of sentences to make clear the two possible senses.

  a) The new traffic control system had failed completely to relieve congestion in the city centre.
  b) The committee considered seriously reprimanding the absentees.
  c) I advise doctors at least to wait for an explanation of the new scheme.
  d) The jury had to examine critically conflicting pieces of evidence.
  e) The person who lies frequently gets caught.
  f) The only woman who was not shouting loudly protested.
  g) Candidates who fail often do not read enough.
  h) I only suggested I should attend as reserve.
  i) If you don't report next week you'll be struck off the register.
  j) She told me when we met we could discuss it.

4. Why is each of the following unsatisfactory in construction?

  a) Two young men today pleaded guilty to attempting robbery with violence in the Central Criminal Court.
  b) The fire was put out before any damage could be done by the fire brigade.
  c) A group of admirers of *Under Milk Wood* have arranged to present this satire of Welsh life in New York.
  d) Wanted: Young Girls to Sew Lace Trimmings on the Fourth Floor.
  e) The Army needs badly trained motor mechanics.

f) We noticed a large placard on the wall of the hut put up specially for new recruits.

g) It was not safe to cross the temporary bridge made by the natives with a horse.

h) We decided to take the road across the moors, instead of going round them to shorten our journey.

i) They followed the huntsmen mounted on horses wearing red coats.

j) (Memorial Inscription) Erected to the Memory of George Baker Drowned in the Thames by his Fellow Directors.

5. Identify and defend the 'split infinitives' in each of the following.

a) The oil lamp my landlady was good enough to still allow me the use of . . .

b) Her intention was to partly cook the joint the night before.

c) Many of us who write books are quite willing to split an infinitive or to half split it or quite split it according to effect. We might even be willing to sometimes so completely, in order to gain a particular effect, split the infinitive as to practically but quite consciously run the risk of leaving the 'to' as far behind as the last caboose of a broken freight train. (Stephen Leacock.)

32 · Proximity – Pronominals

SAMPLE

A] Mr Hobbs reminded his wife that *he* owed *her* five shillings.

   *Mr Hobbs reminded his brother that *he* owed *him* five shillings.

B] *The Romans encountered the barbarians; *they* were well armed.

   *Although I prefer British to American films, I do not dislike *them*.

C] *When the pudding is cooked remove *it* from the oven and switch *it* off.

   *No one could tell the twins apart except their parents, and sometimes *they* had difficulty, until *they* started speaking.

D] *Many people are half asleep when *they* get up, but if *you* have a set time for getting up, *you* will feel fresh. In consequence *he* will not have to rush to get to work.

E] *The subscription was increased without consulting the members; *this* annoyed me very much.

   *The police fought the bandits until *their* ammunition ran out.

   *The headmaster made a change in the fire regulations, the object of *which* was to ensure reasonable safety.

COMMENT

The Principle of Proximity requires that closely related items be placed closely enough together to avoid doubt or ambiguity. Special care is needed in ensuring the proper linkage of Pronominals to the Nominals they represent, since there are often other Nominals near by.

A] The use of the same Pronominal (he/him) for the two men in the second sentence leaves the reader in doubt as to who owed whom.

B] It cannot always safely be assumed that a Pronominal refers to the last-mentioned Nominal. The context suggests that this is so in the second sentence, but probably not in the first.

c] Once a certain Pronominal is used, it will tend to retain the same reference throughout the sentence and perhaps beyond it. Here the writers unwisely expect the two uses of 'it' and 'they' to refer to different Nominals.

D] The same Pronominal should be retained throughout for reference back to the same Nominal.

E] The same principles apply to other forms of Pronominal than the Personal (he, she, it, they, etc.) – e.g. to 'this', 'that', 'these', 'who', 'which', 'that', etc.

EXERCISES

1. Criticize the use of Pronominals in the following sentences and write improved versions of what was presumably intended:

   a) A shark-spotter plane employed by the council apparently failed to see the shark although it was circling over the bathers.

   b) Most of us know someone like that and usually feel bored after spending some time in their company.

   c) The man aimed a blow at my head, which slipped off and hit me on the shoulder.

   d) She probably influenced her brother more than anyone else.

e) He is wearing a red and yellow cap, which is his school colours.

f) She told me that Joe had come, which pleased me.

g) The airship was about to leave the airport. The last person to go up the gangway was Miss Hemming. Slowly her huge nose turned into the wind. Then, like some enormous beast, she crawled along the grass.

h) As the guard went about his duties, he watched him closely, noting the time he came to feed him.

i) Keats's poetry has been so thoroughly discussed by the critics that one can never be quite sure that he is saying anything new.

j) Father might have some potassium chlorate lying around in the garden shed, which he uses for fertilizer.

2. Comment on the following anecdote:

A sergeant told a private: 'This is a hand grenade. You just pull this pin and throw it. Go ahead!' The explosion injured both men. In hospital the private turned to the sergeant in the next bed and asked: 'What happened? I threw the pin just as you said.'

Part Four

ADJUNCTS

33 · *Adnominals*

SAMPLE

	S	V	SC	IO	DO	OC
A]	Toothache	hurts.				
	Toothache	is	an affliction.			
	Toothache	undermines			health.	
	Toothache	causes		people	agony.	
	Toothache	made			grandfather	a tyrant.
B]	Toothache	is	troublesome.			
	Toothache	made			grandfather	bad-tempered.

C] a troublesome affliction; a troublesome toothache.
a bad-tempered tyrant; my bad-tempered grandfather;
bad-tempered people.
the health of the sufferer; general physical health.
all those people who suffer from it.

D] The proposal which the most intelligent supporters of the only other
party worth consideration brought forward was approved.

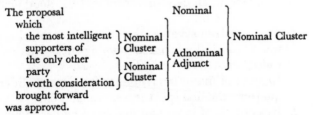

COMMENT

A] In these five basic patterns all items except the Verbs
are Nominals.

B] Complements (both SC and OC) may alternatively be Adnominal (see Sections 15 and 17 above).

C] Though Adnominals are very common as Complements, they are even more common as *Adjuncts*, joining with Nominals to form Nominal Clusters (see Section 9 above). Adnominal Adjuncts may, singly or in groups, precede or follow Nominals, and may each be a single word or a larger word-group.

D] A sizeable Adnominal Adjunct may contain within itself a number of small Nominal Clusters.

EXERCISES

1. Pick out the Nominal Clusters in the following sentences. In each case identify its function (S, SC, DO, IO, OC) and its headword. (Ignore sub-clusters within Nominal Clusters).

a) Many well-known actors attended the funeral of their late colleague.

b) The wedding celebration was the noisiest function that he had ever attended.

c) People from all over the world sent the flood victims gifts of all kinds.

d) The most remarkable item in the whole collection was a beautifully polished shooting-stick containing a rolled umbrella.

e) In spite of many interruptions from many different quarters, the first speaker went on and on.

f) Heavy falls of snow had made the higher mountain passes of the area completely unusable.

g) The clock we had been given hardly ever showed the correct time of day.

h) The foreign-looking man who had aroused so much curiosity had inexplicably disappeared.

i) The new ruler of Ruritania appointed one of his most notorious enemies special envoy to Illyria.

j) The manager of the theatre, who was usually so obliging, was unable to promise him a reasonably good seat in the stalls.

2. Add to the following list ten more Nominal Clusters to illustrate the great variety possible in the size and construction of these items. Underline the headword of each cluster:

> unexpected *invitation*
> *rooms* of moderate size
> several very strange *creatures* with enormous horns
> *people* who live in glass-houses

3. What considerations seem to determine whether Adnominal items in a Nominal Cluster precede or follow the headword? What is rather unusual about clusters such as:

> soldiers three, water enough, the day following, chapter ten, Edward the First, the journey inland, Friday next, the floor below, the way ahead, good men and true.

4. Why do we usually hyphenate Adnominals such as those in the following expressions?

> an out-of-this-world look
> his believe-it-or-not attitude
> devil-may-care behaviour
> a take-it-or-leave-it expression
> reach-me-down clothes

5. The headline 'Girls Plump for New University' has caused amusement. Why?

34 · Types of Adnominal Adjunct

A]

(1)		(2)	
Nominal Cluster		*Nominal Cluster*	
Adnominal	*Nominal*	*Adnominal*	*Nominal*
examination	questions	difficult	questions
question	paper	interesting	paper
paper	hat	old	hat
hat	shops	popular	shops

B]

Nominal Cluster	
Adnominal	*Nominal*
Furniture Shop Blaze	Drama
Atom Injury Law Suit	Claim

COMMENT

A] The Nominals under (1) can also (normally in their Singular form) be used as Adnominals. The normal possibility of Singular and Plural variants (e.g. question(s), hat(s)) and of use with a preceding Nominal Marker (a/an/the, etc.) indicates that these are primarily Nominals in character. The Adnominals under (2) operate primarily as Adnominals and only rarely otherwise; the possibility of variants of comparison (*most* difficult, *less* interesting, old*er*, *very* popular) confirms that these are primarily Adnominals.

B] It is increasingly common in English to form Nominal Clusters using as Adnominals words that are primarily Nominal. Newspapers often do it on a large scale, sometimes at the expense of elegance or even of clarity.

EXERCISES

1. Extend the following series as far as you can by using each Nominal as an Adnominal in the next cluster.

a) reference library
        library book
               book title

b) ground floor
        floor show
               show business

c) shop front
        front door

d) car radio
        radio station

e) gift parcel
        parcel post

2. Try and make up series of clusters (of any length) similar to those in Ex. 1 above but beginning and ending with the same term;

e.g. *flower* garden/garden *flower*
    table model/model kitchen/kitchen *table*

3. Find or invent five newspaper headlines similar to those in Sample B above and containing at least four items each.

35 · Adnominals of Place and Time

SAMPLE

A]	Subject	Verb	Subject Complement
	The enemy	seemed	*everywhere.*
	The emergency	is	*here and now.*

B] The havoc *everywhere* was indescribable.
The people *here* are all members.
The march *home* seemed endless.
The celebration *afterwards* lasted all night.
The day *before* was March 12th.

COMMENT

We shall see later (Section 46) how indication of Place and
Time is usually made through Adverbal constructions.
But a few common Place/Time terms are often used Adnominally, either as Complements (as in A above) or as
Adnominal Adjuncts in Nominal Clusters (as in B). They
are distinguished from the normal single-word Adnominal
in that: (i) in clusters they always follow and could not
normally precede the headword, and (ii) they have no
variants of comparison marked either by suffixes -er, -est
or by more/most/less/least.

EXERCISES

1. Write sentences in which the following are used as
   Complements:
       inside, there, next, later, nowhere
2. Write sentences in which the following are used as Adnominal Adjuncts in Nominal Clusters:
       inside, there, thereafter, above, downstairs.

36 · Genitive (Possessive) Adnominals

SAMPLE

A] the *car*　battery　　　　the *car's*　battery
　the *river* banks　　　　the *river's* banks
　a　*pig*　sty　　　　　　a　*pig's*　sty

a *man* child	a *man's* child
the *sister* ship	my *sister's* ship
the *head* gardener	the *Head's* gardener

B]   + 's   + '

the policeman's wife	a boys' school
policemen's wives	the Boilermakers' Society
children's games	Achilles' heel
Mr Jones's dog	Moses' brother
an ass's head	asses' heads
St James's Park	St James' Church

c] anybody's guess, no one's business, one's health;
my car, his opportunities, her life, its results, your
choice, their replies.

COMMENT

There is no very satisfactory term for the class of forms
here discussed (i.e. Nominals plus 's or just '). 'Possessive'
describes a large number of them, but many others do not
really indicate possession. On the other hand, the traditional 'Genitive' is not in itself descriptive at all.

A] Many words primarily Nominal in character (e.g. car,
river, head) can also, as we saw in Section 34, operate
as Adnominal Adjuncts. With some such words both
the basic form and the Genitive (Possessive) form
(written with 's or just ') can be so used. In clusters such
as the first three it makes little difference which is used.
But in the last three the two forms mark important
differences.

B] The simple ' marks no speech feature; the 's marks the
addition of an s/z sound. Can you see from these two
lists the principle on which we either do or do not add
this sound? Why does it allow both St James's and St
James'?

c] Common Pronominals such as 'I', 'he', 'you', 'it' have separate Genitive Adnominal forms ('my', 'his', 'your', 'its'). Words such as 'one' or 'anybody' resemble Pronominals in meaning, but have Genitive forms similar to those of Nominals.

EXERCISES

1. Find or make up five pairs of clusters similar to those in Sample A above.
2. Find or invent five phrases, like St James'/St James's Park, in which the addition of -s seems to be a matter of personal taste.
3. It is becoming increasingly common nowadays in printed notices, headings and the like to leave out the simple ' after a Nominal ending in -s (e.g. BOYS SCHOOL, LADIES ROOM). Find five more examples of this usage.
4. What is odd about the following sentence from a modern novel:

'We are fugitives from Lady de Moses's,' Sarah said.

37 · Adnominal Phrases and Clauses

SAMPLE

a most skilful *performance*	a *performance* of great skill
two heavily bearded *undertakers*	two *undertakers* with heavy beards
a remarkable *sight*	a *sight* to see
a never-to-be-forgotten *occasion*	an *occasion* that I shall never forget

COMMENT

You probably noticed earlier (Section 33) how in Nominal Clusters the Adnominal Adjuncts sometimes precede and sometimes follow the headwords. The Articles (a, an, the) always, and numbers (two, three, etc.) almost always precede. Other single Adnominals or series of single Adnominals, along with any attachments they may have (e.g. heavily bearded), usually precede. The Adnominals that follow headwords are generally themselves clusters. The commonest types of these are:

Adnominal Phrase: (performance) of great skill/ showing great skill

Adnominal Infinitive: (a sight) to see/(an occasion) to remember

Adnominal Clause: (an occasion) that I shall never forget

The Infinitive construction is normally distinguished by 'to'. The Clause is distinguished by containing its own predication (e.g. I shall . . . forget); it is often introduced by a word such as 'that', 'who', or 'which', though these link-words are sometimes left out (e.g. an occasion I shall never forget).

EXERCISES

1. Separate each Nominal cluster in the following sentences into Headword and Adnominal. Classify the Adnominal Adjuncts as single Adnominal, series of Adnominals, Phrase or Clause.

   a) A thing of beauty is a joy for ever.
   b) The form prize books chosen by the staff proved a very odd selection.

G

c) A short, dark, fierce-looking foreigner whom I did not recognize was sitting at the table.

d) Few people wearing rosettes were to be seen.

e) It was a performance to be admired rather than imitated.

f) A quick goal scored by a team playing energetic football can often undermine the confidence of an opposing team which expects to win easily.

g) The official gave each of us a long form to fill in.

h) Applications for leave of absence should be submitted a week in advance.

i) A representative of the insurance company of your choice will call on you tomorrow.

j) She was the most unconventional, happy-go-lucky, irresponsible young woman I had ever met.

2. Write clusters of similar meaning to the following, replacing the italicized adjuncts with adjuncts in the alternative position (i.e. after the headword instead of before it, or vice versa). State what kind of Adnominal each of your new adjuncts is (i.e. single, series, Infinitive, Phrase or Clause).

a) a *ready-to-wear* suit

b) a problem *to solve*

c) a course *for beginners*

d) this *extremely unpopular* policy

e) all players *who have done this before*

f) a *negligible* proportion

g) these articles *made by machine*

h) the *responsible* person

i) a *never-ending* series

j) the boy *from next door*

3. What is at all unusual about the order of items in the Nominal Clusters in the following sentences?

a) The explanation below refers to the sentence above.
b) The Greeks worshipped the body beautiful.
c) Members present are asked to subscribe to this fund.
d) Tennis proper, as distinct from lawn tennis, is a very ancient game.
e) Tuesday next is the opening night of the performance.

4. Definitions often identify the thing defined through Nominal Clusters, in which the Headword indicates the class of object and the Adnominal Adjuncts before and/or after the Headword indicate differentiating characteristics, e.g.:

An oast-house is a *large brick* kiln *in which hops are dried.*

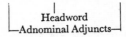

Pick out the Nominal Clusters similarly used in the following definitions, identify Headword and Adjuncts, and state the kind of each Adjunct (single Adnominal, series of Adnominals, Infinitive, Phrase, Clause).

a) A mansion is a large residence.
b) A rebel is a person who resists authority.
c) An igloo is an Eskimo dome-shaped hut made of snow and ice.
d) A shovel is a scooping instrument for shifting coal, earth, etc.
e) An IOU is a signed promise to pay.
f) A manuscript is a document written by hand.
g) A scalpel is a surgeon's small knife shaped for holding like a pen.
h) A punt is a flat-bottomed boat propelled by a long pole thrust against the bottom of a river or lake.

i) Steam is the vapour into which water changes when it is boiled.

j) Optimism is the tendency to look on the bright side.

5. Use the formula of Ex. 4 to define the following items. Underline the Adnominals used to characterize each item and indicate the type of each Adnominal (single, series, Infinitive, Phrase, Clause).

a) a triangle	*f)* a bi-plane
b) a lorry	*g)* blackmail
c) a chauffeur	*h)* poison
d) a hangar	*i)* a pet
e) ink	*j)* ambition

38 · Adnominal Clauses

SAMPLE

A]		Single Adnominal	Nominal Headword
S		High	tides
V	made		
DO		low-lying	fields
OC		extensive	lakes.

B]		Nominal	Adnominal Clause
S		The audience,	which had been waiting impatiently,
V	gave		
IO		the speaker,	whose car had broken down on the way,
DO		a reception	he didn't enjoy.

COMMENT

Any or all of the Nominals in a sentence may have Adjuncts. These Adjuncts may be single Adnominals (as in A), Adnominal Clauses (as in B), or any other kind of Adnominal (e.g. Adnominal Phrases). There is a danger, of course, that – as in the above examples – the repeated use of the same kind of Adjunct will seem mechanical.

Adnominal Clauses commonly begin with link-words such as 'who' (whom, whose, to whom), 'which' (of which, that, etc.), or with such equivalents as 'where' (in the sense of 'in which place') or 'when' (= 'at which time'). Sometimes, as we saw in Section 37 and as we see again in Sample B above, the link-word is left out.

EXERCISES

1. Pick out the Adnominal Clauses in the following sentences. State which headword each qualifies and what function that headword performs in the sentence:

   a) He was a man in whom I had absolute trust.
   b) The type I prefer is no longer being made.
   c) George ignored all the instructions I had given him.
   d) They called the *Titanic* the ship that couldn't sink.
   e) He taught all those who volunteered the rudiments of Russian.
   f) The day you left proved to be a disastrous one for us.
   g) Is there anything we can do?
   h) The thief repaid £500 to those whom he had robbed.
   i) They reached the junction where they had arranged to meet.
   j) Midnight is the hour when ghosts are supposed to walk.

2. Criticize the use of Adnominal Clauses in the following sentences. Rewrite each more effectively.

a) Later there will be a party in the church hall, where children will be able to receive from the vicar who will be dressed up as Father Christmas a present which will be free of charge.

b) The cabinet, which stands on top of the chest of drawers, which is against the wall, still holds the tube of the television set, which merely attracts visitors' attention, the loudspeaker, which I often connect to the gramophone, and a transistor radio receiver which I built into it.

c) This is the piano which we tried to sell to the dealer who works at the shop from which we are buying the new one that is due to be delivered today.

3. Find five newspaper headlines containing Adnominal Clauses.

4. Make up five sentences containing Adnominal Clauses introduced by different forms of the link-word 'who' (to/from/of whom, of/from whose, etc.) and five introduced by 'which' or some form containing 'which' (e.g. to which). What general principle seems to determine whether a who-form or a which-form is suitable? In what way does the following sentence appear to be an exception to that principle?

He looked like a solicitor – which he was.

39 · Adnominals – Proximity

SAMPLE

A] A *lump* appeared on his forehead *about the size of a hen's egg.*
The *body* of the swimmer, *which had been in the water several days,* . . .
A *man* with a brick, *who was standing outside a jeweller's shop,* . . .

B] *He was carrying an object covered with white spots *about the size of a hen's egg.*

*I pulled my hat on to my head, *which was much too big for me.*

*She recognized a friend of her mother, *who used to visit them often.*

COMMENT

A] Adnominal Phrases and Clauses can sometimes quite safely be separated from their Headwords – or *Antecedents*, as they are usually called. Such separation is sometimes made easier with Clauses by the link-word, the character of which may prevent association of the Clause with an intervening Nominal. Thus 'which' tends to refer back to a 'thing', 'who' to a person.

B] A Nominal coming between Antecedent and Adnominal item can, however, attract the Adnominal to itself and thereby cause ambiguity. It is important to observe the principle of proximity, which requires items linked closely in thought to be kept close enough together in words to avoid the slightest misunderstanding.

EXERCISES

1. Identify Antecedent, link-word and Adnominal Phrase or Clause in each of the following sentences. Where (as in some but not all) the principle of proximity is not observed, rewrite the sentence more satisfactorily.

a) This was a development for which he was not prepared.

b) A sailor was dancing with a wooden leg.

c) The pages of the register which he kept for private transactions had been torn out.

d) Next came a mother with a very young baby who was pushing a pram.

e) I bought a book about an escape from a prison camp called 'Stalag Luft XII'.

f) The only explanation of their absence that I could think of was sudden illness.

g) I always buy my newspapers at the shop next to the police station in which cards, magazines, and fancy goods are displayed.

h) An investigation was carried out of remarkable thoroughness.

i) Bows and arrows which had poisoned tips were their only weapons.

j) The girl was followed by a small poodle wearing jeans.

2. Why is each of the following sentences more or less ambiguous? In place of each write a pair of sentences expressing the two possible meanings.

a) It is the end of a lecture that is important.

b) He was wearing a cap and gloves which he had borrowed from his brother.

c) The government made a slight alteration to the Act which was designed to help smaller firms.

d) It was the mother of the girl whose voice I had recognized.

e) He eventually found the key to the padlock which had been mislaid.

3. From a Sunday newspaper: 'Our report last week included the ambiguous remark: "One of the actors involved, Mr H. V. Hodson, Editor of the *Sunday Times*, whose future is far from clear at the moment, said. . . ." We express our apologies to Mr Hodson.' Explain the ambiguity and show how it could have been avoided.

40 · *Restrictive and Non-restrictive Adnominal Clauses*

A] (written) The two climbers, who were feeling exhausted, went back.

(spoken) ²The two ³clímbers² →⁺ ²who were feeling exhausted² →⁺ ²went back¹ ↘

B] (written) The two climbers who were feeling exhausted went back.

(spoken) ²The ³two ²clîmbers who were feeling exháusted² →⁺ ²went back¹ ↘

COMMENT

Sentence A is about a pair of climbers; Sentence B is about two from a larger group of climbers. The main statement – 'the two climbers went back' – makes fair sense in A without the Adnominal Clause, which merely adds 'extra' information. But in B the Adnominal Clause is tied much more closely to its Antecedent 'climbers'; it *restricts* the main statement to those two climbers who were exhausted; without it the situation is misrepresented.

In writing, this important distinction is made by using a pair of commas round the non-restrictive, but not the restrictive, clause. In speech, there is a corresponding difference of intonation pattern. Most speakers keep the who-clause separate in the non-restrictive (A) pattern by rising to pitch 3 and using major stress on /³clímbers/ and by pausing slightly in the level transition (² →⁺ ²) to 'who'.

EXERCISES

1. Punctuation marks are deliberately omitted from the following sentences. Read each sentence aloud with two different intonation patterns; then write them out properly punctuated and explain the difference in meaning involved.

   a) the marines who had mutinied were court-martialled
   b) all the children who were in the basement escaped alive
   c) the yachts which were anchored near the sea wall were damaged
   d) he picked out from the group all the doctors whose experience would be most useful in the emergency
   e) the ban applies only to motor-cycles which are noisy and smelly

2. What is wrong with the following sentences? Re-write them so as to make clear the intended meaning.

   a) It is useless giving books to children, who can neither write nor read.
   b) There are no private schools in Russia, where it is possible to pay for one's education.
   c) He hated lessons, which involved writing essays.
   d) Reminders were sent to all the members, whose subscriptions had not been paid.
   e) Scissors, which have been allowed to get very rusty, are not easy to sharpen again.

41 · Adverbals

A]

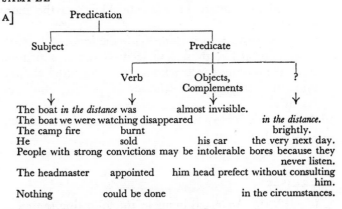

```
                    Predication
                         |
        ┌────────────────┴──────────────────┐
     Subject                             Predicate
                              ┌──────────────┼──────────────┐
                           Verb          Objects,           ?
                                       Complements
        ↓                ↓                ↓               ↓
```

The boat *in the distance* was   almost invisible.
The boat we were watching disappeared   *in the distance.*
The camp fire   burnt   brightly.
He   sold   his car   the very next day.
People with strong convictions may be intolerable bores because they
                                                         never listen.
The headmaster   appointed   him head prefect without consulting
                                                               him.
Nothing   could be done   in the circumstances.

B] *In the circumstances*, nothing could be done.
C] i) *Ready or not*, you'll have to come now.
       No one raising any objection, he helped himself.
    ii) The result, *I think*, was quite satisfactory.
    iii) Tomorrow is Friday, *isn't it?*
D] *Though he hated doing it*, he *quickly* hid the parcel *under the table*.

COMMENT

A] In the first sentence 'in the distance' is an Adnominal
Phrase expanding the Nominal 'boat'. In the second
sentence the same phrase expands, not the Nominal
'boat', but the Verb 'disappeared'. It may therefore be
called here an *Adverbal*. The other sentences show how
such Adverbals may expand the Verb alone (e.g.
burnt – brightly) or the whole Predicate (e.g. appointed
him prefect – without consulting him) or even the
whole Predication (e.g. Nothing could be done – in the

circumstances). These last very general Adverbals are sometimes called Sentence Adverbals.

B] Sentence Adverbals may occupy various positions. Other Adverbals are also often movable, though naturally those attached to specific items such as the Verb alone tend to be less movable than the more general ones.

c] It is convenient to include with Sentence Adverbals constructions like those italicized. A sub-classification into (i) absolute constructions, (ii) interjected clauses, and (iii) confirmatory clauses is possible but not essential.

D] A single Verb may have several Adverbals, of varying kind and position.

EXERCISES

1. Identify the Adverbal items in the following sentences and indicate as clearly as you can the kind of information each gives.

a) By nightfall they had explored the island thoroughly.
b) Politicians should think more and talk less.
c) With extreme care he poured the acid into the bottle.
d) As they could get no reply, they pushed a note through the letter-box.
e) I shall resign if you don't co-operate with me.
f) He hurried home to hear the news.
g) The scientists learned a great deal from the experiment, even though it failed.
h) The fog thickened, so that they could see hardly a yard in front of them.
i) He lay quite still, like a corpse.

j) To everyone's delight, a small man carrying a large ladder fell flat on his face in Holborn the other morning.

2. An Adverbal may, of course, be attached to any kind of Verb:

– to a Simple Verb	– He *reached* the office	
– to a Verb Cluster	– He *used to reach* the office	by nine o'clock.
– to a Phrasal Verb	– He *got to* the office	
– to a Phrasal Verb Cluster	– He *used to get to* the office	

In each of the following sentences pick out the Adverbal item and the Verb it expands. State which of the above four categories the Verb belongs to and what kind of information the Adverbal gives.

a) We shall be going soon.
b) We shall be going away tomorrow.
c) George reached the required standard without difficulty.
d) If possible, we shall fly there.
e) He persevered, though he had no hope of succeeding.
f) Nobody ought to be so sure of himself that he does not even listen to the opinions of others.
g) She went on with what she was doing as if nothing had happened.
h) The fan may not have been working where the explosion occurred.
i) He braked hard, to avoid hitting the pram.
j) The house being scheduled for demolition, we shall not be able to stay here much longer.

42 · *Movable Adverbals*

A] *At midday* he went to the bank.
He went *at midday* to the bank.
He went to the bank *at midday*.
B] The house *badly* needs painting.
*The house needs painting *badly*.

COMMENT

A] Adverbals are much more movable in position than
Adnominals. One reason for this is that there are
usually fewer Verbs in a sentence than Nominals, so
that the risk of a wrong Adverbal–Verbal linkage is
generally less than that of a wrong Adnominal–
Nominal linkage. Another reason is that, as we have
seen, the Adverbal often expands not just the Verb but
also the rest of the Predicate or even the whole Predication. The varying positions for Adverbals often serve to
make slight variations in emphasis.
B] Occasionally – e.g. where there is more than one
Verbal item (needs, painting) – there is only one satisfactory position for an Adverbal.

EXERCISES

1. Change the emphasis but not the essential meaning of
each of the following sentences by moving an Adverbal:

a) He slowly made his way home.
b) They well know the danger.
c) Children are all too often spoiled by fond parents.

d) He returned the ball to the bowler with a quick flick of his wrist.

e) If you are tired, why not rest for a while?

f) The old man still dug the garden, though crippled with rheumatism.

g) On the shore they found the remains of a bonfire.

h) He switched on his headlights, so that the rescue workers could see the overturned lorry.

i) I shall eventually go abroad.

j) She was wearing on her head what looked like a flower-pot.

2. Explain how in each of the following an Adverbal item is so placed as to convey a very unlikely meaning. Re-write them so as to convey the meaning probably intended.

a) Bank Staff Forced to Kneel by Raider.

b) Body Seen Floating through Library Window.

c) The police were searching for clues to the murder with a magnifying-glass.

d) He hid the letter with his heart beating wildly in his pocket.

e) He could see the workers pulling down the pig-sty from the roof.

3. Change the meaning of each of the following sentences by moving an Adverbal item.

a) In time I shall finish.

b) We agreed on Friday evening to have a party.

c) He immediately made up his mind to resign.

d) The firm paid well all those who worked for it.

e) Happily she did not die.

f) Although injured he tried to continue playing hard.

g) He kept in the workshop all the pieces he had found.

h) He knew he ought to be on his way as soon as he woke up.

i) As she was sleeping soundly, she didn't hear her brother being thrashed.

j) He quickly decided to go over the programme once more.

4. Explain how the placing of an Adverbial causes ambiguity in each of the following sentences. Write pairs of sentences to make clear the two possible meanings.

a) Do you intend seriously to discuss the problem?

b) The canopy failed completely to protect the spectators from the rain.

c) They agreed cheerfully to co-operate with us.

d) I did not follow your meaning precisely because you talked at too great length.

e) We decided deliberately to be late.

43 · Adverbials and Adnominals – Item-order

SAMPLE

A] *Nearly* everybody fainted.   Adnominal ⎱ Word
    Everybody *nearly* fainted.   Adverbal ⎰

B] The official *with the flag* made no sign.   Adnominal ⎱
    The official made no sign *with the flag*.   Adverbal ⎰ Phrase

C] The marshes *where the bird-watchers used to hide* have been drained.   Adnominal ⎱
    The marshes have been drained *where the bird-watchers used to hide*.   Adverbal ⎰ Clause

COMMENT

The same item may sometimes operate either as Adnominal or as Adverbal. In pairs of sentences such as the above only the item-order differentiates between the two uses. In such cases an Adverbal is hardly more movable than an Adnominal, though in the second sentences of B and C the Adverbal might just possibly come first instead of last.

EXERCISES

1. Pick out the Adverbal or Adnominal item in each of the following sentences; state which it is; then write another sentence illustrating the alternative use of the same item.

   a) The woman behind the counter smiled.
   b) A strange man appeared in the doorway.
   c) The ship disappeared in the distance.
   d) The only man present laughed.
   e) Scarcely a sound could be heard.

2. Example:

   He watched the ship *with a telescope*.   – Adverbal
   He watched the ship *with the tall masts*. – Adnominal

   Compose further pairs of sentences like this. The following phrases may be useful and may suggest other possibilities.

in a bad mood	/	in an old car
under the table	/	under suspicion
with pleasure	/	with a pleasant outlook
by inches	/	by drowning
without petrol	/	without salt

H

3. Make up pairs of sentences, like those in the Sample, using each of the following items in one as Adnominal, in the other as Adverbal:

> with an umbrella
> only
> where they were
> fast
> over the top

44 · *Adverbals and Adnominals – Ambiguity*

SAMPLE

A] I could see the man *from the insurance* — Adnominal
   company.
   I could see the river *from the upstairs flat*. — Adverbal
   *I could see the man *from the upstairs flat*. —   ?
B] The game continued *slow*. — Adnominal
   The game continued *slowly*. — Adverbal
   *She looked *hard*. —   ?

COMMENT

A] The possibility of the same item being used either Adnominally or Adverbally can create ambiguity. In the first two sentences context selects one meaning rather than the other. But in the third two alternative meanings are possible.

B] There are very many pairs – such as 'slow/slowly' – in which the -ly ending distinguishes the Adverbal form from the Adnominal. But a few terms, such as 'hard' ('hardly' has a special sense), do not have this distinction and therefore may prove ambiguous.

EXERCISE

1. Identify the ambiguous item in each of the following sentences. Then write pairs of sentences, using it first as a clear Adverbal, then as a clear Adnominal.

   a) I could see the man from the upstairs flat.
   b) She looked hard.
   c) We saw them with the telescope.
   d) The club will be open to members only from Tuesday to Friday.
   e) They finished the race with Saucy Sally several lengths behind.
   f) 'I want to try on that suit in the window.'
   g) Nobody knew who had murdered the old man with a walking stick.
   h) We left our tent by the river.
   i) He opened the cash-box under the desk.
   j) Did he really paint the picture in the attic?

2. Explain the difference in grammar and in meaning between: She reached home safely.
   and: She reached home safe.

45 · Degree-words

SAMPLE

A] The boat pitched *slightly*.
   The prizes were *fairly* distributed.
   They behaved *strangely*.
   Surprisingly, no one complained.

B] He felt *slightly* sea-sick.
   He recovered *fairly* quickly.
   The enemy were *strangely* silent.
   The time passes *surprisingly* fast.
C] They must have worked *very* slowly.
   The statue had been painted *bright* red.

COMMENT

A] The italicized words are clearly Adverbals, expanding
   Verbs or – in the fourth sentence – a whole predication.
B] The same words here expand, not Verbs, but Adnominals or Adverbals. This usage differs from that in
   A in that here the words indicate degree rather than
   manner and have fixed positions before their Adnominals or Adverbals. To mark the difference, let us
   call them *Degree-words*.
C] Degree-words such as 'very' cannot normally be used as
   ordinary Adverbals; we do not say 'The boat pitched
   very.'

EXERCISES

1. Pick out the Degree-words in the following sentences
   and state whether they qualify Adnominals or Adverbals:

   a) The weather proved remarkably fine.
   b) I have never seen a more surprising change of for-
       tune.
   c) They turned back rather reluctantly.
   d) Earthquakes are distinctly rare occurrences.
   e) Their friends called less and less often.
   f) The ship approached dangerously near.
   g) Our well was completely dry most of last summer.
   h) He was in one of his unusually cheerful moods.

i) They lived near a very dangerous crossroads.
j) Life became more and more difficult.

2. A sentence such as 'The rebels needed *more* modern weapons' is ambiguous in writing. In speech transition and stress would indicate either

'more modern   weapons'
(Degree-word + Adnominal + Nominal) or:
'more   modern weapons'
(Adnominal + Adnominal + Nominal).

Make this difference clear in writing by composing two sentences for the two different meanings.
Then do the same for the following sentences:

a) The mermaid is a pretty strange creature.
b) I would have preferred less old-fashioned furniture.
c) There were even more ancient cottages in the next village.
d) Less serious illness has been treated at home.
e) Even more remarkable results were reported from the towns.

46 · Adverbal Clauses

SAMPLE

He stood quite still . . .

. . . where he was.	Place:	where?
. . . while the police searched him.	Time:	when?
. . . as though he was in a trance.	Manner:	how?

... because he dare not move.	Reason:	why?
... if anyone approached him.	Condition:	on what condition?
... so that he could listen carefully.	Purpose:	for what purpose?
... so that he was hardly noticed.	Result:	with what result?
... though he longed to move.	Concession	in spite of what?
He stood as still ...		
... as if he were made of stone.	Degree:	how (much)?

COMMENT

The labelled items are all Clauses, each containing its own Predication. They illustrate the main kinds of information that Adverbals (not only Clauses but also Phrases and simple Adverbals) commonly convey. The classification is intended only as a rough guide; some Adverbal items do not fall cleanly within any one of the classes; and some classes overlap – Degree, for instance, could be treated as a kind of Manner.

EXERCISES

1. Write nine sentences to show how Adverbals other than Clauses (i.e. Phrases and single words) can be used to indicate Place, Time, etc.
2. Adverbal Clauses can sometimes be compressed to Phrases by ellipsis – that is, by leaving out words (including the Verb) that can be taken for granted. E.g.:

    Although (they were) exhausted, they staggered on.

    Re-write the following sentences, substituting Adverbal Clauses for the elliptical Adverbal Phrases. State what kind of Adverbal Clause each is.

a) Although anxious to get away, he waited an hour for me.

b) While undressing, we chatted idly.

c) I'll let you know, if necessary.

d) The plan worked exactly as intended.

e) Unless thoroughly rehearsed a play is not worth presenting.

f) Examinations are necessary, however unpleasant.

g) When finished it will look more impressive.

h) If well enough I shall attend the meeting.

i) He was never to be found when wanted.

j) The young men were staggering about as if drunk.

3. Adverbal Clauses are often more or less equivalent to Adverbal Phrases that are not elliptical, e.g.:

The convict stayed *where he could not be seen*.
The convict stayed *in hiding*.

Rewrite each of the following sentences, substituting an Adverbal Phrase for the Adverbal Clause, or vice versa. State what kind of Adverbal each item is.

a) You must not leave unless you are allowed to.

b) Despite the wind he went out sailing.

c) After shutting the shop she went to the cinema.

d) While the animals were performing the band went on playing.

e) He shouted and screamed like a madman.

f) When we had finished the painting we went home.

g) No smoking was allowed, lest there should be an explosion.

h) There were traces of fire at the bandits' last camping site.

i) He always wore a sun-helmet, to protect him from sunstroke.

j) The sea was so rough that the lifeboat could not be launched.

4. Write pairs of sentences of more or less equivalent meaning, one containing an Adverbal Clause, the other an Adverbal Phrase, introduced by the following pairs of items:

Adverbal Clause	Adverbal Phrase
a) as though . . .	like . . .
b) so that . . .	to . . . (Infinitive)
c) since . . .	-ing . . .
d) although . . .	regardless of . . .
e) no sooner . . . than . . .	on . . . immediately . . .
f) so far as . . .	to . . .
g) if . . .	but for . . .
h) though . . .	in spite of . . .
i) lest . . .	for fear of . . .
j) while . . .	during . . .

5. Find ten newspaper headlines containing Adverbal Clauses (e.g. Khrushchev Acts *as Big Four Talk*) and state as precisely as possible the nature of the Adverbal's function (e.g. Time).

6. Example:

Although he was a wealthy man, he lived in a small hotel.
Before/until/when/while/after he was a wealthy man, . . .
As/because/since he was . . .

Sometimes a number of different relationships between two ideas can be indicated simply by joining them with different link-words. Join the following pairs of items in as many different ways as seem reasonably possible:

a) she was his wife/she stayed at a hotel
b) the match was over/the crowd swarmed on to the pitch

Make up three further sets of similar examples.

47 · *Phrasal Verbs and Adverbal Phrases*

SAMPLE

A]

	The dispatch-rider		
Simple Verb	entered	came *in*	Phrasal Verb
Simple Adverbal	hurriedly	*in* a great hurry	Adverbal Phrase

B]

	The wind		
Simple Verb	blew	blew *down*	Phrasal Verb
Adverbal Phrase	*down* the chimney	the chimney	Direct Object

COMMENT

A] The same words that as Particles combine with Verbs to make Phrasal Verbs can often begin Adverbal (and Adnominal) Phrases. In the latter case they are usually known as *Prepositions*.

B] Normally the context indicates whether such a word is a Particle ending a Phrasal Verb or a Preposition beginning an Adverbal Phrase. But occasionally, as here, both readings are possible; the word 'squints'. In speech, intonation patterns differentiate between the two possibilities by varying stress and transition:

The wind → blew dówn the chimney.
The wind bléw → down the chimney.

EXERCISES

1. Identify the 'squinting' Particles in each of the following
sentences and quote the Phrasal Verb and Adverbial
Phrase to which each might belong. Then write pairs of
sentences to make clear the two possible meanings.

 a) The loudspeaker woke everyone up in the attic.
 b) The frightened horse ran into the guards' van.
 c) The detective looked over the desk.
 d) He stood by his friend throughout the trial.
 e) He fell on the picnic hamper.

2. Example:

 The butler *waited on* the guests. (S + Phr. V + DO)
 The butler *waited/on* the doorstep. (S + V + Adv.
  Phr.)

Write similar pairs of sentences using the following items:

a) wait for	*f*) blow up
b) deal with	*g*) turn on
c) run over	*h*) call for
d) look up	*i*) go into
e) fall over	*j*) do for

3. Comment on anything odd or interesting in the following:

 a) Doctor: 'Lie down and I'll just run over your chest.'
 b) He ran up a steep bill. Then, leaving the restaurant,
  he ran up a steep hill to the Town Hall.
 c) He waited for the next bus for an hour and a half.
 d) Pets Fly Off With Queen Mother.
 e) We shall not stand for any arrangement that expects
  old people to stand for more than an hour.

4. Write pairs of sentences showing how the following
Particles can be used either in Phrasal Verbs or in Adverbal Phrases:

for, up, with, on, across, at, over, into, by, down.
(Useful Verbs for this purpose include: come, get, go,
look, run, stand, turn.)

5. Example:

They *ran out of* petrol. (Phrasal Verb + DO)
They *ran out* of the fog. (Phrasal Verb + Adverbial
Phrase)

Make up pairs of sentences, similar in pattern to the
above, based on: stand up for, come up to, get on with,
go back on, go in for, look down upon, look up to,
come in for.

48 · Participle Phrases

SAMPLE

A] 1. In tears
   2. Weeping bitterly   } she sank to the floor.
   3. Overwhelmed by grief

B] 1. Without hesitation
   2. Pausing hardly at all   they dashed into the
   3. Impressed by the need   blazing warehouse.
      for haste

C]   *Preposition Phrase*   *Participle Phrase*

	Continu*ing*	Complet*ed*
A.1. In tears	A.2. Weep*ing* bitterly	A.3. Overwhelm*ed* by grief
B.1. Without hesita- tion	B.2. Paus*ing* hardly at all	B.3. Impress*ed* by the need for haste

COMMENT

A, B] Of the two Preposition Phrases, A.1. is Adnominal (= tearful), B.1. is Adverbal (= unhesitatingly). The Participle Phrases have more or less parallel functions. The Adnominal/Adverbal distinction is fairly though not absolutely clear between A.2. (weeping) and B.2. (pausing), but perhaps more arguable with the remaining pair. A fuller context is needed to decide whether 'overwhelmed by grief' is primarily an Adnominal expansion of 'she' or an Adverbal expansion of 'sank' (i.e. indicating why she sank). Conversely, 'impressed by the need for haste' may be Adverbal (indicating why they dashed) or Adnominal (suggesting their state of mind).

c] Traditionally the two kinds of Participle are called Present and Past, despite the fact that they can both be used in reference to past, present, or future time. Continu*ing* and Complet*ed* perhaps describe their functions more accurately. The -ing form is standard; the Completed Participle ends in -ed for most Verbs, but not for all (e.g. burn*t*, beat*en*, sw*u*m, been).

EXERCISES

1. Make up two more sets of sentences like the Sample above.

2. Pick out the Participle Phrases in the following sentences. Identify the Participle as Continuing or Completed and discuss whether each Phrase is Adnominal or Adverbal (or either) in character.

   a) The birthday cake, decorated with icing-sugar, looked almost too good to eat.

   b) Hearing a cry for help, the life-guard plunged into the sea.

c) Dressed all in black, the mourners stood at the grave-side.

d) Dressed all in black, the mourners found the heat unbearable.

e) Carrying an umbrella and brief-case, the stock-broker looked quite out of place on the bathing-beach.

3. Identify the Participle Phrase in each of the following headlines, state its nature and function, and then find five more examples:

a) Man Entombed at Agadir Had Store of Food.
b) Firemen Die Fighting Blaze.
c) Youth Clinging to Cliff Saved by Children.
d) Defeated by One Vote, Mayor Resigns.
e) Man Holding Toy Gun Robs Bank.

49 · Dangling Participles

SAMPLE

A] * A sailor was dancing *with a wooden leg*.

*The accused was sentenced to death for murdering an old lady *at Winchester Assizes*.

B] *A spotter-plane kept a look-out for sharks *circling over the bay*.

On failing the entrance examination his father sent him to a boarding school.

*I bought a book about an escape from a prison camp *called The Wooden Horse*.

Covered with grease the water did not seem unduly cold to the swimmer.

COMMENT

A] In discussing Proximity (Section 31 above) we noted the importance of placing Preposition Phrases near enough to the relevant Nominal or Verbal to avoid a wrong association.

B] The same principle applies to Participle Phrases. If they are left 'dangling' they may attach themselves to the wrong item.

EXERCISES

1. Explain the weakness of each of the sentences in the Sample above and rewrite it more satisfactorily.
2. Identify the dangling Participle in each of the following sentences and rewrite the sentences to make clear the meaning presumably intended:

 a) We saw the Eiffel Tower flying from London to Paris.

 b) On re-reading *Treasure Island*, Stevenson seems to me an exceptionally fluent story-teller.

 c) While driving along the High Street, a cat darted out in front of him.

 d) When assured that his brother was safe, relief overcame his anger.

 e) On entering the house the atmosphere always seems to welcome the visitor.

50 · *Infinitive Adjuncts*

A] This is essentially a book *to study*.　　　　　– *Adnominal*
　He settled down *to study*.　　　　　　　　　– *Adverbal*
　The gramophone was not easy *to carry*.　　　– *Modifier*
B] She had little time *to practise her service*.　– *Adnominal*
　She got up early *to practise her service*.　　– *Adverbal*
　He got up too late *to have any breakfast*.　　– *Modifier*
c] Bison are animals *to be treated with respect*.　– *Adnominal*
　He left work early *to be vaccinated*.　　　　　– *Adverbal*
　The star was not bright enough *to be seen*　　– *Modifier*
　　without a telescope.

COMMENT

A] Like Preposition Phrases and Participle Phrases (Section 48), Infinitives can operate as Adjuncts of various kinds. As Adnominals they may expand Nominals (a book to study = a textbook). Adverbally, they may expand Verbs (settled down to study = settled down studiously). In the third usage they may expand Adjuncts (Adnominal or Adverbal); for lack of a better term they may in this function be called *Modifiers*.
B] Similar uses are possible with Infinitive Phrases, in which the Infinitive has its own Direct Object.
c] Many Infinitives have Passive forms (to be + Completed Participle); these, too, can act variously as Adjuncts.

EXERCISES

1. Identify the Infinitive item in each of the following and describe its function:

    a) It was too early to think of going to bed.
    b) Room to Let.
    c) A taxi-driver is not a person to be trifled with.
    d) The chairman rose to quell the disturbance.
    e) The price was too high to be acceptable to the committee.
    f) The noise grew and grew to fill the whole building.
    g) There was no opportunity to discuss the latest developments.
    h) The bus conductor hurried to pick up the little old lady.
    i) Some spectators found the display tedious to watch.
    j) The coronation was an occasion to be remembered.

2. Example: *portable*

    The radio set was quite *easy to carry.*

Write sentences using Infinitive constructions instead of the following words. State in each case the kind and function of the Infinitive item:

    deplorable, avoidable, memorable, fearsome, probable, illegible, manageable, immeasurable, dangerous, praiseworthy.

3. Find five more words which can be used similarly to 'portable' in Ex. 2 above.

4. Write sentences in which Infinitive items are Adjuncts to the following:

    a chance, permission, too windy, paused, fascinating.

Part Five

NOMINALS

---

51 · Nominal Phrases – Infinitives, Gerunds

A] *To become an expert at anything takes time.* — Subject

Most of us hate *to be continually interrupted.* — Direct Object

The only alternative was *to wait a while.* — Subj. Complement

B] *Where to begin* was the problem. — Subject
Nobody knew *what to do next.* — Direct Object
The problem was *where to begin.* — Subj. Complement

C] *Becoming an expert* takes time. — Subject
Most of us hate *continually being interrupted.* — Direct Object

The only alternative was *waiting a while.* — Subj. Complement

D] The doctor heard *him cough.* (Compare: told him *to* cough)
The doctor heard *him coughing.* (Compare: heard *his* coughing)

I

COMMENT

A] Infinitives, alone or in Phrases, may be used not only as Adjuncts (see Section 50), but also as Nominals, operating as Subjects, Objects or Complements.

B] A Nominal Phrase may consist of an Infinitive compounded with a question-word such as 'where', 'what', 'how'.

C] Parallel usages are possible with Phrases based on the -ing form, known in this case as *Gerunds*. Nominal Phrases with Infinitive or Gerund differ from Nominal Clusters in that, instead of comprising basic Nominal + Adjunct, they are based on Verbal items.

D] It is convenient to treat Direct Object + Infinitive without 'to' and DO + Gerund as special kinds of Nominal Phrases.

EXERCISES

1. Identify the Nominal Phrases in the following. Indicate whether they are based on Infinitives or Gerunds, and what function they fulfil.

a) Nobody likes to feel unwanted.
b) Most children enjoy swimming.
c) The rest of the work was picking fruit.
d) To interrupt without seeming rude requires great tact.
e) Nobody knew when to start operations.
f) Peeling potatoes is a dreary job.
g) The remedy was to start again.
h) He was wondering what to do next.
i) The animals seemed to resent being put on show.
j) How to stop laughing I didn't know.

2. Pick out from the following the Phrases based on -ing forms and state whether they are: (i) Nominal (i.e. based on a Gerund), or (ii) Adnominal or Adverbal (i.e. based on a Continuing Participle).

   a) Wearing a thick overcoat, he stepped out into the blizzard.
   b) Realizing that he must soon be discovered, the murderer gave himself up.
   c) He hated wearing a thick overcoat.
   d) The patrol, suspecting an ambush, sent a scout ahead.
   e) Going out straight after a hot bath is a sure way to catch cold.
   f) The greatest hazard would be climbing down the cliff in the dark.
   g) The passengers walked up and down the platform, fuming and fretting at the delay.
   h) Growing cabbages is not the most interesting part of gardening.
   i) They had intended for some time having the room decorated.
   j) The bus-driver, not having a watch, did not realize that he was running ahead of schedule.

3. Explain the ambiguity in the following. (Reading aloud should help.)

   a) Flying planes can be dangerous.
   b) She hated cooking sherry.
   c) But she liked stewing steak.
   d) They asked questions about my spending money.
   e) He wasted no time on moving pictures.

SAMPLE

A] The captaincy
To become captain
Becoming captain } was his secret ambition.
*That he should become
captain*

B]
Some writers prefer {
anonymity.
to remain anonymous.
remaining anonymous.
that they should remain anonymous.

C]
The chief problem
was {
famine.
to find food.
finding food.
that food was extremely scarce.

COMMENT

Nominal items, whether used as Subjects (as under A), as
Direct Objects (as under B), as Complements (as under C)
or in other ways, may be single words or phrases or – as in
the fourth of each set – Clauses. Like other Clauses these
are distinguished by containing their own predication.
One of the commonest introductory words to a Nominal
Clause is 'that'; sometimes, especially when the Clause
acts as Direct Object after a Verb like 'said', the introductory 'that' is omitted.

EXERCISES

1. Pick out the Nominal Clauses in the following sentences and say whether they operate as Subjects, Direct Objects, Indirect Objects, Subject Complements, or Object Complements:

   a) What impressed me was the accuracy of the detail.
   b) He asked me why I wanted to leave.
   c) The proposal is that a new club should be formed.
   d) Nobody gave what he was saying the slighest attention.
   e) Hours of toil failed to make the garden what he planned.
   f) Her friends told her she ought to protest.
   g) That we should all fail is inconceivable.
   h) What I have I hold.
   i) Nobody knew whether the game had been cancelled.
   j) (A sign in an American bar)

> I ain't what I've been.
> I ain't what I'm going to be.
> I am what I am.

2. Rewrite the first five sentences in Ex. 1 above, substituting Nominal Phrases or Clusters for the Nominal Clauses.

3. Why is the following sentence ambiguous? Write a pair of sentences to illustrate clearly the two meanings possible.

   Do you think that one will do?

4. Identify the Nominal Clauses in the following headlines and state the function of each.

   a) Bonn Says Allies Approved Plan.
   b) Youth Took Car, Say Police.

    c) Women Prove Village is Alive.
    d) Frightened Man Tells Court Why He Lied.
    e) Court Rules Steel Strikes Must End.

5. Find or invent five more headlines containing Nominal
   Clauses.
6. A few link-words (e.g. if) may introduce either Nominal
   or Adverbial Clauses. The context usually prevents ambiguity, but exceptionally two readings are possible.
   Explain the grammar and the meaning of the two
   possibilities in the following sentences. (In one or two of
   them punctuation could be used to mark one of the
   meanings.)

    a) Please report when you get back.
    b) You should ask your teacher if you are not making
   good progress.
    c) He claimed the right to be told immediately whether
   it was convenient or not.

53 · *Nominal Clauses – Reported Speech*

SAMPLE

A] 1. The referee said, 'The pitch is unfit for play.'
      'The pitch is unfit for play,' the referee said.
      'The pitch is unfit for play,' said the referee.
      'The pitch,' said the referee, 'is unfit for play.'
      'The pitch,' the referee told the two captains, 'is un-
      fit for play.'
  2. 'When you're ready,' said the coach-driver.
  3. 'In a few minutes' time,' explained the waiter.
  4. 'Upstairs,' replied the commissionaire.

B] 1. The referee said that the pitch was unfit for play.
   2. The coach-driver said he could leave when they were ready.
   3. The waiter explained that dinner would be served within a few minutes.
   4. The commissionaire told them that the cloakroom was upstairs.

COMMENT

A] The Verb 'say' and similar Verbs such as 'tell', 'explain', etc. naturally operate very often with 'sayer' and 'words said' in a S + V + DO pattern. In Direct Speech, when the actual utterance is given exactly, intonation in speech or inverted commas in writing make variations of the normal order of items quite possible. (See also Section 27.) The Direct Object utterance may be a complete sentence, a clause, a phrase, or a single word.

B] The corresponding Reported Speech pattern is more rigid. The normal item-order prevails and the utterance is usually phrased as a Nominal Clause, commonly (though not invariably) introduced by 'that'.

EXERCISES

1. Write sentences corresponding to the following, using Reported Speech and underlining the Nominal Clauses functioning as Direct Objects. (Where necessary invent supplementary information from an imagined context.)

   a) Soldier Says: 'I Heard Screams.'
   b) 'Where,' demanded the master, 'is the blackboard?'
   c) 'The spare ones are painted blue,' he explained.
   d) Errol Flynn Says: 'I Was with Castro.'
   e) 'Why don't you try the side door?' the policeman asked us.

f) 'Do you play golf or cricket?' the officer demanded
   of each recruit.
g) 'Yesterday,' she admitted, 'I took the day off.'
h) The witness answered: 'No, I was in bed at the time.'
i) 'I left the papers here this morning,' the clerk in-
   sisted.
j) 'Shall we go on waiting or not?' I inquired.

2. The omission of 'that' before a Nominal Clause Direct
   Object can sometimes cause ambiguity. Demonstrate
   the ambiguity of each of the following sentences by
   writing out the two sentences possible with 'that'.

   a) She told me when she finished her studies she would
      marry me.
   b) He said before leaving he would answer all the
      letters.
   c) The actor admitted without prompting he would
      never have remembered his lines.
   d) The manager said when tempers had cooled the con-
      test could be resumed.
   e) We decided since you were here you ought to join the
      club.

54 · *Apposition*

SAMPLE

We English are sometimes thought to be unfriendly people.
Winston Churchill, the wartime Prime Minister, was later
   knighted.
The city of *Canterbury* is in *the county* of *Kent*.
His intention, to protect the society's reputation, was praise-
   worthy.

He stated clearly *his intention*, namely *that the society's reputation should be protected.*

It was desirable *that the society's reputation should be protected.*

COMMENT

Two Nominal items (words, phrases, or clauses) can share a function merely by being placed alongside or near each other – in *Apposition*, it is called. Sometimes, as with 'of' in the third and 'namely' in the fourth of the above samples, a link-word is used.

Either of the two apposed items could operate more or less satisfactorily on its own, e.g.:

He stated his intention.

He stated that the society's reputation should be protected.

Sometimes, as in the last sample, 'it' is used as a kind of stand-in for the first Nominal item, so that the second and more important one may occupy the stronger final position.

EXERCISES

1. Identify the pairs of Nominal items in Apposition in the following sentences:

    a) He could not settle the problem whether to apply or not.

    b) It dawned upon her that her leg was being pulled.

    c) The island of Jamaica is in the British West Indies.

    d) This is the last will and testament of me, Alexander Anderson.

    e) No one paid any attention to the wife, poor soul.

    f) It is impossible to get toothpaste back into its tube.

    g) Peter the Painter was a notorious murderer.

    h) The question whether the headmaster should be invited was discussed at length.

i) He persisted in pressing his argument, that we should all resign.

j) The next process, fitting the roof on, was a delicate operation.

2. It is often possible – and economical of words – to use a phrase in Apposition instead of an Adnominal Clause, e.g.:

James, *who plays the piano expertly*, cannot sing a note.
James, *an expert pianist*, cannot sing a note.

Rewrite the following sentences, using appositional phrases in place of the Adnominal Clauses.

a) I voted for Jane, who makes excellent speeches.

b) The caretaker, who had fought in the Boer War, kept strict order in the playground.

c) They were specially interested in the automatic hair-cutting machine, which had only recently been invented.

d) He put Geography, which was the subject he liked best, at the top of his list.

e) Thomas Edison, who invented the gramophone, has a lot to answer for.

3. Comment on the structure of the following sentence from the preface to *The Return of Hyman Kaplan*. The American author, Leo Rosten, is doubting the wisdom of attempting a second story about Kaplan, for:

'The locale could scarcely be less inspiring: a classroom, a classroom of a beginner's grade, a classroom of a beginner's grade in a night school, a classroom of a beginner's grade in a night school for adults, a classroom of a beginner's grade in a night school for adults presided over not by a rich, juicy character, such as Samuel Johnson or Scaramouche, but by a terribly staid teacher named Parkhill.'

Part Six

STRUCTURES

---

55 · Relationships and Constructions

A] i) car/pre-war
   ii) Description
   iii) Appositional Phrase
   iv) Our car, *a pre-war model*, will probably not pass the
       new test.
B] i) competitors/spiked running-shoes
   ii) Identification
   iii) Clause
   iv) The competitors *who wore spiked running-shoes* were
       disqualified.
c] i) collect fragments/re-assemble
   ii) Time
   iii) Participle Phrase
   iv) *Having collected all the fragments* he carefully stuck the
       vase together again.

COMMENT

Given two suitable notions (i) and a relationship (ii),
there is often a choice of constructions for combining
them. In the Sample above one construction (iii) is
specified for use in a sentence (iv). Any one relationship
may be expressed through various constructions; for
example, Purpose may be expressed by Clause (We stayed

at home *so that we should avoid the crowds*) or Infinitive (. . . *to avoid the crowds*). Conversely, a single type of construction may serve to express various relationships; for example, an Adnominal Clause may serve Description or Identification; a Preposition Phrase may convey Identification (the man *from the insurance company*), Reason (*because of the heavy rain*, . . .), Purpose (*for private use*), Concession (*despite the rain*), etc.

EXERCISES

1. Construct sentences according to the following specifications. Underline item (iii) in each sentence.

- a) i) heavy rain/match cancelled
     ii) Result
     iii) Clause
- b) i) heavy rain/match not cancelled
     ii) Concession
     iii) Clause
- c) i) heavy rain/match will be cancelled
     ii) Condition
     iii) Clause
- d) i) swimmer/fourteen hours
     ii) Description
     iii) Participle Phrase
- e) i) previous engagement/invitation not accepted
     ii) Reason
     iii) Preposition Phrase
- f) i) hid/slip away later
     ii) Purpose
     iii) Participle Phrase
- g) i) seats/cushions
     ii) Identification
     iii) Preposition Phrase

h) i) thunderstorm/second half of game
    ii) Time
    iii) Clause

i) i) horse/bolted
    ii) Description
    iii) Clause

j) i) extra work/complete the job
    ii) Condition
    iii) Preposition or Participle Phrase

k) i) stared/hypnotized
    ii) Manner
    iii) Preposition Phrase

l) i) final took place/Wembley
    ii) Place
    iii) Preposition Phrase

m) i) huntsmen conspicuous/'pink' coats
    ii) Description
    iii) Participle Phrase

n) i) rope broke/climbing precipice
    ii) Time
    iii) Preposition Phrase

o) i) smoked glass/eclipse of sun
    ii) Purpose
    iii) Infinitive Phrase

2. Rewrite any ten of your answers to Ex. 1 above, substituting a different kind of construction (e.g. a Clause
instead of a Phrase) for the underlined item, and making
any other changes that become necessary. State what
kind of construction the new item uses.

3. Make up four answers to the question 'Where is the key
to the cash-box?', each beginning 'I've put it . . .' and
indicating place by, in turn:

a) a single word
b) a single short phrase
c) a series of two or three phrases (e.g. as if the key had been put in a specially safe place)
d) a clause (e.g. as if the key had been deliberately hidden from the questioner)

56 · Subordination

SAMPLE	*Subordination:*
A] The cross-examination was expertly handled. It lasted only half an hour.	None
B] i) The cross-examination, *which was expertly handled*, lasted only half an hour.	– by Clause
ii) The cross-examination, *which lasted only half an hour*, was expertly handled.	– by Clause
C] The cross-examination, *lasting only half an hour*, was expertly handled.	– by Participle Phrase
D] The cross-examination, *in expert hands*, lasted only half an hour.	– by Preposition Phrase
E] The *expertly handled* cross-examination lasted only half an hour.	– by Adnominal Phrase
F] The *half-hour* cross-examination was expertly handled.	– by single Adnominal
G] i) The cross-examination, *a half-hour affair*, was expertly handled.	– by Apposition
ii) The cross-examination, *an expertly handled affair*, lasted only half an hour.	– by Apposition

COMMENT

Two connected ideas, such as those in A, can be combined in a single sentence in various ways, according to which one is treated as subordinate to the other and according to how the writer wishes to distribute emphasis. It is not often that such a wide range of alternatives as B–G above is available, but commonly a choice can be made from two or three constructions. It has been suggested that 'it is not too great an exaggeration to say that skill in subordination is the first requisite of a successful writer'.

EXERCISES

1. Combine the following pairs of separate ideas in single sentences of the patterns indicated by the index letters taken from the Sample.

   a) The change of scenery was skilfully managed.
      It took only two minutes.
      B (i), B (ii), C, D, E, F, G (i), G (ii).
   b) The secretary's report was carefully written.
      It covered six pages.
      B (i), B (ii), C, E, F, G (ii).
   c) The garage withstood the full force of the gale.
      It was extremely well-built.
      B (i), C, E, G (ii).
   d) The book was almost unreadable.
      It was printed on very poor paper.
      B (i), B (ii), C, D, E, G (i).
   e) Her dress had red and yellow stripes.
      It could be seen from a considerable distance.
      B (i), B (ii), C, D, E, G (ii).

2. Combine the following pairs of separate ideas in single sentences of as many of the patterns shown in the

Sample as seem appropriate. State which pattern is used in each of your sentences.

a) The porter was carrying two large trunks.
He was bent almost double under the load.
b) The preparations were extremely thorough.
They covered every detail.
c) The chairs were well-designed.
They improved the appearance of the room.
d) Many modern cars have very powerful engines.
They can accelerate with remarkable speed.
e) The trial lasted several months.
It was a long-drawn-out affair.

57 · Multiple Items

SAMPLE

A] *Jack and Mary* lent *Bill and Alice* their *car and trailer*. — Nominals

Julius Caesar *came, saw, and conquered*. — Verbs

Many male film-stars are *tall, dark, and handsome*. — Adnominals

Slowly, heavily, but relentlessly, the enormous gates closed. — Adverbals

You seem to be *with but not of* us. — Prepositions

B] They tackled the job *with vigour, though not with much hope of success*. — Preposition Phrases

Soaked to the skin but still hoping to find it, he dived in again. — Participle Phrases

He decided *either to resign from the firm or to ask for a transfer*. — Infinitive Phrases

c] I understood *that you were the singer and*   – Nominal
   that she was the pianist.   Clauses

If I feel better, if my parents agree, and if   – Adverbal
   time permits, I shall join you to-   Clauses
   morrow.

The only candidate *I voted for but you*   – Adnominal
   voted against was elected.   Clauses

COMMENT

The main categories of item, whether basically single
words (as in A), phrases (B) or clauses (C), can operate in
pairs, trios, or larger combinations. Various link-words,
such as 'and', 'but', 'though', 'either . . . or', are commonly used in forming such combinations, which may
conveniently be called Multiple Items.

EXERCISES

1. Complete the following sentences by adding a word or
   cluster to make up a Multiple Item. State what kind of
   Multiple Item each then is.

   a) He played games energetically but . . .
   b) Though I have known you a long time and . . ., I
       shall not be able to recommend you for this job.
   c) You seem to be sympathetic but . . . about the pro-
       posal.
   d) He seemed destined always to seek rather . . .
   e) Screaming, . . . and . . ., the teenagers climbed on to
       the stage.
   f) Hunting, . . . and . . . are aristocratic pursuits.
   g) Association football, which began in England
       and . . ., is less popular than it used to be.
   h) He tackled the job with confidence but . . .
   i) The difficulty was that time was short and . . .
   j) Expenditure has increased, . . ., and . . .
   K

2. Write sentences in which the Multiple Items specified
are used.

a) Two Phrasal Verbs joined by 'but'.

b) Three simple Participles.

c) Two Adnominal Clauses introduced by 'whom'.

d) Two Infinitives used with 'neither . . . nor'.

e) Three Adverbial Preposition Phrases, not all beginning with the same Preposition.

3. Find five newspaper headlines to illustrate five different
kinds of Multiple Item.

58 · Harnessing Multiple Items

SAMPLE

A] *He transported the equipment in a caravan drawn by
a car or horse-drawn.

                    a car

  i) – in a caravan drawn by   or

                    a horse

               by a car

  ii)– in a caravan drawn   or

               by a horse.

B] *At his new school he found himself studying French,
Trigonometry, and playing the piano.

                      French,

  i) – found himself studying Trigonometry,
                       and

                      Music.

             studying French and Trigonometry

  ii) – found himself   and

          playing the piano.

c] *He told the stranger that the house was not his and about the ghost.

$$
\text{– that the house}\quad
\begin{cases}
\text{was not his} \\
\text{and} \\
\text{was haunted by a ghost.}
\end{cases}
$$

D] *He was afraid of neither death nor of torture.

i) He was afraid
$$
\begin{cases}
\text{neither of death} \\
\text{nor of torture.}
\end{cases}
$$

ii) He was afraid of
$$
\begin{cases}
\text{neither death} \\
\text{nor torture.}
\end{cases}
$$

E] *The shepherd stood by the fold into which the sheep were to be gathered and held.

$$
\text{– the fold}\quad
\begin{cases}
\textit{into} \text{ which the sheep were to be gathered} \\
\text{and} \\
\textit{in} \text{ which they were to be held.}
\end{cases}
$$

F] *His job is to record changes of address, telephone numbers, and occupations.

i) – to record
$$
\begin{cases}
\text{occupations,} \\
\text{telephone numbers,} \\
\text{and} \\
\text{changes of address.}
\end{cases}
$$

ii) – to record changes
$$
\begin{cases}
\text{of address,} \\
\text{of telephone numbers,} \\
\text{and} \\
\text{of occupation.}
\end{cases}
$$

COMMENT

Nobody would think of harnessing together a horse and a cow. Similarly, in constructing sentences, items harnessed together (i.e. Multiple Items) should be of the same pattern. The above six samples are all unsatisfactory; they exemplify what the famous Fowler brothers called 'defective double harness' or 'unequal bedfellows'.

The alteration needed is to make the items harnessed together parallel in construction. A, B, and C are straightforward examples. D reminds us of the care needed with constructions involving dual link-words such as 'either . . . or', 'both . . . and', 'rather . . . than', etc. In E a rather cumbersome expansion is necessary because of the two different Prepositions appropriate to the two Verbs ('gathered *into*' but 'held *in*'). F is ambiguous. It is not clear whether 'changes of' belongs solely to 'address' or to telephone numbers and occupations as well.

EXERCISES

1. Rewrite the following sentences so as to improve the harnessing of Multiple Items:

   a) John's behaviour made his brother suspect and angered him.

   b) I was pursued by a policeman and a tracker dog ran after me.

   c) The effects of the new tax were not only felt by the workers, but their wives also suffered from it.

   d) She was captain of both hockey and of netball.

   e) Not only were the slaves sold like cattle but also severely beaten.

   f) If the book is not wanted, it is understood that the borrower will either buy it or will return it.

   g) This was the man of whom he had heard and been warned.

   h) The policeman reported that the house had been broken into and on the smashed window-panes.

   i) He was fond of collecting cigarette cards, foreign stamps, and noting train-numbers.

j) The answers were either printed at the back of the book or in handwriting.

2. Comment on the unsatisfactory harnessing in the following.

a) All old men and women ought to be evacuated from the danger area.

b) The only spectators were a woman carrying a small baby and a large policeman.

c) By a scientific approach I mean that absence of prejudice and open-mindedness which characterizes the work of a good scientist.

d) Death was often a blessed relief from the misery and fear of war.

e) He had a large collection of illustrated magazines and books.

59 · Clause Analysis

SAMPLE

	Clauses Main	Subordinate	Type of Sentence
A] The spectators applauded.	1 only	0	Simple
The spectators clapped, shouted, and stamped their feet.	2 or more	0	Compound
The spectators, who were deeply impressed, applauded.	1 only	1 or more	Complex
The spectators, who were deeply impressed, clapped, shouted, and stamped their feet.	2 or more	1 or more	Compound-Complex

Subordinate Clauses

B] The spectators, *who were deeply impressed,* applauded.   Adnominal

The spectators applauded *long after the curtain had come down.*   Adverbal (Time)

The spectators realized *that they had seen a remarkable performance.*   Nominal (Direct Object)

C] The spectators, who were deeply impressed, realized that they had seen a remarkable performance and applauded long after the curtain had come down.

Main Clause. The spectators realized

Adnominal Clause expanding 'spectators'. who were deeply impressed

Nominal Clause DO of 'realized'. that they . . . performance

Main Clause. and applauded

Adverbal Clause of Time expanding 'applauded'. long after the curtain had come down.

COMMENT

A] The principal grammatical parts of sentences are Main and Subordinate Clauses. Sentences without Subordinate Clauses are called Simple (one Main Clause only) or Compound (more than one Main Clause). The addition of one or more Sub Clauses makes a Simple into a Complex sentence, a Compound into a Compound-Complex sentence.

B] As we have seen, there are three classes of Sub Clause, operating as Adnominals, Adverbals, or Nominals. Adnominal Clauses normally expand a preceding (antecedent) Nominal. Adverbal Clauses normally expand Verbs (indicating Time, Place, Purpose, etc.) or Adjuncts (indicating Degree, Manner, etc.). Nominal Clauses may perform any of the normal Nominal functions (Subject, Object, Complement, Apposition).

C] The component clauses of a sentence may be listed and classified according to their function and their linkage with each other.

EXERCISES

1. Analyse, after the pattern of Sample C, the following sentences. Allocate each sentence to one of the types listed in Sample A.

a) There are young people who under-rate the hard-
   ships of unemployment because they have not ex-
   perienced the difficult times through which older
   people have lived.

b) It is a law of nature that what goes up must come
   down.

c) Before we could reach him, he had untied the rope
   and let the animal free.

d) Whatever you say is unlikely to be understood.

e) Many people are only too willing to criticize their
   local council, but few are able to help it to function
   better.

f) Car-owners who have not long held a driving-licence
   ought at first to avoid roads where traffic is exceptionally heavy.

g) If you are prepared to work hard for the examination you propose to take next year, and if you let me
   know the titles of the books you are studying, I will
   do my best to help you.

h) It was very clear that he had no intention of keeping
   the promises he made when he first arrived.

i) Though they had been rehearsing for several months
   and knew their parts thoroughly, they acted the play
   as if they had hardly read it before.

j) The wallpaper was hanging in strips from the wall
   where the damp had got in and the ceiling threatened
   to collapse at any moment.

2. Analyse the following sentence (from a speech in
   Anouilh's comedy *Thieves' Carnival*) into clauses. Comment on anything odd in the arrangement of clauses
   and suggest what effect the dramatist is aiming at.

   Lady Hurf: . . . Send one attendant after her, send
   another attendant to let us know, and put a third

in your place to tell us where you've gone so we can pick you up on the way home if we should happen to be passing.

3. Find in a newspaper a sentence containing at least four Clauses and analyse it in the above way.

60 · Clause Structures

SAMPLE

A] Nero fiddled while Rome burned.   Main → Sub
   While Rome burned Nero fiddled.   Sub ← Main
B] We noticed   Main
   that the door was locked   ↙   ↘
   but the windows were open   Sub + Sub
C] Nobody knew   Main
                                        ↓
   what had happened   Sub
                                        ↓
   before the crash occurred.   Sub
D] As we approached   we noticed   Sub ← Main
   that the door was locked   ↙   ↘
   but the windows were open.   Sub + Sub
E] Though the plane was crowded nobody Sub ← Main
      knew   ↓
   what had happened   Sub
                                        ↓
   before the crash occurred.   Sub
F] She chose a hat   wore it with a dress Main   Main
                  but   ↓   +   ↓
   that suited her   that clashed with it. Sub   Sub

COMMENT

A subordinate clause is normally dependent on an item in another clause. This other clause may (as in A) come before or after. Variations of order, number, and ranking of clauses allow a considerable range of permutations, of which the above are a few examples.

In B two subordinate clauses are equally dependent on a Main Clause item ('noticed'). In C, which also has one Main and two Sub Clauses, the second Sub Clause is dependent on the first Sub Clause.

D and E correspond to B and C, with a third Sub Clause added before the Main Clause.

Further examples could be devised, not only with more Sub Clauses but with more than one Main Clause (as in F).

EXERCISES

1. Make up a further set of samples similar to A–F above.
2. Some of the following sentences have similar structures to those exemplified above; others represent different permutations of the same elements. Identify the clause structure of each.

   a) The audience was quite unaware of what had gone on just before the curtain rose.
   b) By the time the orchestra had finished the overture, everything was again in order.
   c) Since you insist and since we are not likely to meet again for some time, I agree to your proposal.
   d) Nobody noticed that the door was open and the cat had disappeared.
   e) If he had a scar on his face, he was probably the man who robbed the bank while the fire was raging.

f) This is the dog that chased the cat that ate the rat that ate the corn that lived in the house that Jack built.

g) He picked up an axe that lay nearby and hacked at the tree that was blocking the road.

h) Though heavy rain was falling they struck camp and cycled off.

i) Whatever happens and wherever you go, don't forget to write to me.

j) Before he left he told me that he would call on my uncle, who lived in Ontario, and would give him my best wishes.

61 · Sentence Analysis

SAMPLE

	Main Pattern	Sub Clauses	Notes
1. Drew and Gibson	1. S		Multiple S
went on.	V		Phrasal V
2. They	2. S		
were	V		
eager to reach the camp.	SC		Adn. + Infin. Phr.
3. They	3. S		
did not give	V		
the Indian	IO		
a thought.	DO		
4. But the Indian	4. S		
still followed behind	V		V + Adverbals
like a dog			Adverbal Phr.
which,			introd. Adnom. Cl.
though it has been driven away,		Adverbal	Concession
refused to desert its masters.		Adnominal	DO = Infin. Phr.

5. He	5. S		
knew	V		
that the men would always find food,		Nominal	DO (1st)
and that,	} DO		introd. Nom. Cl.
as long as he followed them,		Adverbal	Condition? Time?
he could not starve.		Nominal	DO (2nd)

COMMENT

Most sentences (though by no means all) are constructed on one or other of the basic patterns. The first stage of analysis is to establish this main pattern. Any item of the basic pattern may itself be a word-group – e.g. a Nominal Clause, a Phrasal Verb, an Infinitive or Participle or Pre-position Phrase. The basic items provide a framework for such other items as may be built into the sentence as expansions of some kind.

The further the analysis is pushed, the greater the possibility of variation or overlap in classification. For instance, in the fifth sentence of the Sample, 'as long as he followed them' is certainly Adverbal in character, but might be thought to indicate Time (in the sense of '*while* he followed them') or Condition ('*provided that* he followed them') or perhaps a mixture of the two. Similarly, 'refused to desert its masters' (sentence 4) might be treated as V 'refused' + DO 'to desert its masters', or as V 'refused to desert' + DO 'its masters'. These differences are not so much faults in the system of analysis as reminders that the living language, though it must be in some degree systematic if it is to remain intelligible, must sometimes break through the restraints of any rigid system if it is to remain alive.

EXERCISES

1. Analyse the following advertisement in similar fashion to the Sample above.

I'M THE RIGHT PERSON TO ASK

If I had space in this advertisement I could write a treatise on indigestion. I know. I get it. I get indigestion because I like good food; because I worry about totally unimportant things; because I rush around much more than I should.

I may get indigestion but I am not so foolish as just to sit there and suffer from it.

I've learnt always to carry a couple of SOOTHEY tablets about with me. They always do the trick. In fact these new ones are even better than the ones I used to get years ago.

2. Analyse similarly:

a) A few hours later we saw in the distance two men on small ponies, wearing the same sort of clothes. We slowly began to feel uncomfortable and went on without waiting for them. Long after dark we came across a tent. Here we were lucky as it was inhabited by a pleasant nomad family, who hospitably invited us to come in and gave us a special fireplace for ourselves. In the evening we got talking about robbers. They were, it seems, a regular plague. Our host had lived long enough in the district to make an epic about them.

b) Suddenly I looked round and saw with some alarm a lot of wild-looking cattle coming slowly out of the bush towards the river. I walked on as if I was quite indifferent to them; but they did not attempt to conceal their interest in me. The bulls, in fact, as soon as they saw me, began to come towards me, and a good many others followed them. Now, I do not suppose there was any real danger; there were not nearly enough to tread me down from mere curiosity, as the bush herds sometimes did to men on foot. But they looked wildish, and I confess I was thoroughly frightened. I thought that perhaps I had actually reached Mount Gibraltar and these were the celebrated wild cattle.

62 · Balanced Sentences

SAMPLE

A] There was cricket on the sand, and sand in the spongecake, and sandflies in the watercress, and foolish mulish religious donkeys on the unwilling trot. (Dylan Thomas)

B] Night fell; the stars came out; all was quiet.

C] He stopped the car and examined the engine.

COMMENT

Sentences such as these, made up of series of more or less equally stressed clusters, are called *Balanced Sentences*. The last item of the series tends to carry a little more weight than the others, because the final position is commonly the most emphatic. In A the writer is deliberately trying to convey the manner in which a series of recollections passes through his mind. The effect of B is more staccato, rather like a sequence of sharp hammer blows. C makes a much duller impression; if the situation had been more urgent more emphasis might have been directed towards the latter part (e.g. As soon as the car stopped, he examined the engine). Clearly a balanced series of more or less equal statements runs the risk of monotony. Balanced Sentences are effective only if the balanced items deserve more or less equal emphasis.

EXERCISES

1. Why is the use of balanced sentences effective in the following:

a) (Huckleberry Finn is making his escape from the cabin in which his 'pop' has locked him up.)

I took the sack of corn meal and took it to where the canoe was hid and shoved the vines and branches apart and put it in; then I done the same with the side of bacon; then the whiskey-jug; I took all the coffee and sugar there was and all the ammunition; I took the wadding; I took the basket and gourd; took a tin dipper and a cup, and the skillet and the coffee-pot. I took fish lines and matches and other things. I cleaned out the place.

b) Behold my servant, whom I uphold;
Mine elect, in whom my soul delighted;
I have put my spirit upon him:
He shall bring forth judgement to the Gentiles.
He shall not cry, nor lift up,
Nor cause his voice to be heard in the street.
A bruised reed shall he not break,
And the smoking flax shall he not quench.

(Bible)

2. Find three more short passages which rely for their effectiveness mainly on the use of balanced sentences.

63 · *Loose and Suspended Sentences*

A] I shall stop your pocket-money if you break another
window and don't own up to it.
If you break another window and don't own up to it, I
shall stop your pocket-money.
B] He at last staggered out of the smoke-filled room,
gasping for breath and holding his hands over his eyes.
Gasping for breath and holding his hands over his eyes,
he at last staggered out of the smoke-filled room.

COMMENT

In the first sentences of these pairs, the Main Clauses are
stated first. In the second sentences, the Main Clauses
follow the Subordinate Clauses. When, as in the latter, the
Main Clause is placed finally, it tends to acquire strong
emphasis. The effect is, as it were, of building up to a kind
of climax which is held back to the end; that is why this is
called a *Suspended Sentence*. The reverse construction, as in
the first sentences, is called *Loose*; here the main point is
made first and further matter is added, with a tendency to
'tail away' in a declining movement.

EXERCISES

1. Classify the following sentences as Loose, Suspended, or
Balanced. Discuss the effect in each case of using the
chosen type of construction.

   a) Though it was his birthday and though he had been
   looking forward for weeks to celebrating it at the

club with his friends, he agreed to stay in and look
after the baby.

b) They stood rooted to the spot, afraid to make the
slightest movement and waiting tensely for the
animal to move away.

c) (The meal seemed endless.) The soup was so hot that
they had to wait for it to cool; the fish was so full of
bones that they had to eat it with great care; the
meat was so tough that every mouthful had to be
thoroughly chewed; and the sweet was so slippery
that only the tiniest amounts could be held in the
small spoons provided.

2. Make up a set of three sentences similar to those in
Ex. 1 above.

64 · Mixed Sentences

SAMPLE

A] Directly he could walk without a stick,	Advbl Cl.	⎫ Suspended
he descended into the town	Main Cl.	⎬
to look for an opportunity to get home.	Advbl Phr.	⎭ Loose
B] Picking up the stick	Advbl Phr.	Suspended
he sharpened the end	Main Cl.	⎫ Balanced
and pushed it into the hole,	Main Cl.	⎬
listening attentively all the while.	Advbl Phr.	⎭ Loose

COMMENT

The single sentence need not be Loose, Suspended, or Balanced throughout; it would be dull if only these three movements were possible. Commonly the movement of a sentence, as shown above, changes from one type to another.

EXERCISES

1. Analyse the following sentences on the lines of the above Sample:

  a) Settling down into bed and pulling the blankets right up over his head, he lay still until he eventually fell asleep.

  b) The wind dropped, the sun came out and the waves subsided, so that the holidaymakers were able at last to enjoy what remained of the day.

  c) When the time seems right, the funds are available, and the members all agree, we shall launch the campaign.

2. Pick out five sentences from a book or newspaper and analyse them similarly to the above.

65 · Repetition of Patterns

SAMPLE

(From Virginia Woolf's *Flush*, in which life is seen and smelt through the eyes and nose of a spaniel)

A] Door after door shut in his face as Miss Mitford went downstairs; they shut on freedom; on fields; on hares; on grass; on his adored, venerated mistress. . .

L

B] He smelt the swooning smells that lie in the gutters; the bitter smells that corrode iron railing; the fuming, heady smells that rise from basements. . . .

c] Setting one thing beside another, he had arrived at a conclusion. Where there are flower-beds there are asphalt paths; where there are flower-beds and asphalt paths, there are men in shiny top-hats; where there are flower-beds and asphalt paths and men in shiny top-hats, dogs must be led on chains.

COMMENT

A] The sequence of 'on'-phrases represents the chain of simple notions in the dog's mind. Their repetition builds up bit by bit the sense of loss.

B] The repetition of Nominal Clusters in which the head-word 'smells' is amplified by a preceding Adnominal and a following Adnominal Clause suggests the rich variety of exciting smells reaching the dog's nose.

c] The rather laborious and complicated expansion of the Adverbal Clauses reflects the slow progression of the dog's 'thinking'.

EXERCISES

1. What patterns or structures are repeated in each of the following quotations from *Flush*? What is the purpose of the repetition?

  a) The routine of leave-taking was intolerably pro-longed; but at last Mrs Jameson, Mr Kenyon, and even Miss Mitford had risen, had said good-bye, had remembered something, had found something, had reached the door, had opened it, and were – Heaven be praised – gone at last.

b) Mr Barrett, the seven brothers, the two sisters, the butler, Wilson and the maids, Catiline, Folly, Miss Barrett and Flush all went on living at 50 Wimpole Street, eating in the dining-room, sleeping in the bedrooms, smoking in the study, cooking in the kitchen, carrying hot-water cans and emptying the slops from January to December. The chair-covers became slightly soiled; the carpets slightly worn; coal dust, mud, soot, fog, vapours of cigar smoke and wine and meat accumulated in crevices, in cracks, in fabrics, on the tops of picture-frames, in the scrolls of carvings.

c) He went in and out, up and down, where they beat brass, where they bake bread, where the women sit combing their hair, where the bird-cages are piled high on the causeway, where the wine spills itself in dark red stains on the pavement, where leather smells and harness and garlic, where cloth is beaten, where vine leaves tremble, where men sit and drink and spit and dice. . . .

d) Up the funnel of the staircase came warm whiffs of joints roasting, of fowls basting, of soups simmering. Mixing with the smell of food were further smells – smells of cedarwood and sandalwood and mahogany; scents of male bodies and female bodies; of coats and trousers; of crinolines and mantles; of curtains of plush; of coal dust and fog; of wine and cigars.

e) Indeed, when the world seems tumbling to ruins, and civilization rocks on its foundations, one has only to go to Wimpole Street; to pace that avenue; to survey those houses; to consider their uniformity; to marvel at the window curtains and their consistency; to admire the brass knockers and their regularity; to observe butchers tendering joints and cooks

receiving them; to reckon the incomes of the inhabi-
tants and infer their consequent submission to the
laws of God and man – one has only to go to Wimpole
Street and drink deep of the peace breathed by
authority in order to heave a sigh of thankfulness
that, while Corinth has fallen and Messina has
tumbled, while crowns have blown down the wind
and old Empires have gone up in flames, Wimpole
Street has remained unmoved. . . .

2. What pattern is repeated in the following, and to what
effect?

a) In the years since Mr Kaplan and Company first
asserted their peculiar dominion over my life, I have
been asked many questions, about him and about my-
self – by baffled friends who thought I had a nerve
confiding to them that 'Leonard Q. Ross' and I were
two and the same; by teachers throughout the land
who were beginning to talk to themselves because of
Kaplans or Pinskys of their own; by entirely innocent
students who had been condemned to institutions of
learning and were wrestling doomed matches with
the cunning and slippery syntax of English; by
critics trying to shore up the sea wall between their
fantasies and mine; by refugees, from Europe and
the Orient, who simply could not believe that anyone
not himself a refugee could possibly understand the
tortures they had endured studying the language invented by Torquemada.

(Rosten: *The Return of Hyman Kaplan*)

b) 'My lord, the sentiments that you express and the
demeanour which you have evinced are so greatly at
variance with the title that you bear and the lineage
of which you spring that no authority that you can

exercise and no threats that you are able to command
shall deter me from expressing that for which, however poor and inadequate my powers of speech, all
these of whom and for what I am what I am, shall
answer to it for the integrity of that, which, whether
or not, is at least as it is. . . .'

(S. Leacock)

c) In fact, it was he who arranged that you should be
kidnapped, who sent you the bogus message, who in-
veigled you into staying at the Splendide Hotel, who
shot at me on the ship, who cunningly won your confidence as soon as he came on board at Alexandria,
and prevented me from warning you.

(R. Fuller)

3. What two constructions are repeated in the following
opening of a letter proposing marriage?

Dear Miss Blank Blank,

Ever since I first had the honour of meeting you
beside the sawdust pile behind the sawmill at the
Y.M.C.A. picnic on the 18th June ult., I have
realized that I entertain for you a feeling which is
different from any feeling which I have hitherto entertained for anyone for whom I have entertained a
feeling. . . .

(S. Leacock)

4. What construction is deliberately repeated in the following sentence? What does the repetition suggest
about the behaviour described?

But before that, the infantry had already arrived,
debouching from the 'Place de Ville' on the crowd's
rear long before the cavalry officer could have reported to the officer of the day, who would have dis-
patched the orderly, who would have summoned the

batman, who would have interrupted at his ablutions
and shaving the adjutant, who would have waked the
town-major in his night-cap, who would have tele-
phoned or sent a runner to the infantry commander
in the citadel.

(W. Faulkner)

5. What is the outstanding feature of the sentence-structure in the following passage? What does it suggest
about Tim, who often visits the circus-ground at the
animals' feeding-time? In what way does this style of
writing prepare the reader for what follows, when Tim
lets the lion out and takes it for a walk?

> Samson was the lion. It was near his cage Tim
> always stood. It wasn't a big cage. It barely fitted the
> body of the lion. Tim felt his own limbs cramped
> when he looked at the cage. Samson wasn't like a lion
> you would see in books or a picture. His mane was
> not bushy. It was nearly all worn away. There was
> only a bit of it left around his head, up near his ears.
> He didn't roar either.

6. Write a short paragraph based on one of the following
situations. Try to suggest the quality of the situation –
e.g. the feeling of the person concerned – through repetition of a suitable construction.

   a) A housewife discovers a heavy fall of soot just after
   she has spring-cleaned the drawing-room.
   b) Searching for something lost.
   c) A husband waiting restlessly and anxiously outside
   the maternity ward where his wife is having their
   first baby.

   d) A small child has just discovered the delights of watching his reflection in a mirror.

   e) A half-starved tramp is given a lavish meal.

7. Extend the following by adding information organized on the pattern indicated:

   a) He had never received such a monstrous collection of Christmas presents: a back-scratcher from Aunt Edna, a shaving-mug from . . .

   b) He was trapped. In front of him raged the swollen river. Behind him, . . .

   c) She could hardly recognize the street in which she had lived as a child. The houses were dilapidated, the garden overgrown, . . .

   d) He looked round at the staid, respectable faces of his four school-mates. Could that really be Higgins, who had let loose an army of mice in the Chemistry Lab. ? Was that Skipton, who had . . .

   e) The jury were convinced of his guilt by his shifty appearance, by . . .

   f) Having checked my bicycle brakes, having . . ., I felt thoroughly prepared for the trip.

   g) Young animals quickly learn to fend for themselves, to . . .

   h) It is advisable to start learning to skate while your limbs are still supple, while . . .

   i) Hated by his enemies, . . ., he decided to kill himself.

   j) They agreed to take a number of precautionary measures: to light a camp fire, to . . .

8. The following sentence is unsatisfactorily constructed. Re-write it, using two sentences based on the same pattern.

If you keep a book a week overdue, a fine of two-pence is laid on until when three weeks is due, you get a card to your house telling you to return it as soon as possible.

9. Where a sentence pattern is repeated to no obvious purpose, it may become not only ineffective but monotonous. This seems to have happened in the following extracts. Rewrite them in more varied style.

a) Leaving my typewriter I put on my hat and coat in readiness to go home. As I opened the door a cloud of fog pushed its way in. Pulling my collar up I stepped forward. Craning my neck to see where I was going, I came to a corner and remembering that I turned right I did so and there before me was the familiar bus station. Walking on I eventually found my bus and embarked. Finding that all the seats on the lower deck were occupied I went upstairs and found a seat next to the window.

b) This lawn is not suitable for use. This is caused by several trees which are close to the park's eastern boundary which put a shade over it for several hours of the early morning, which leads to a loss of the benefit of the sun which is very important to the life of the turf.

SAMPLE

In that instant,	Phrase	
in too short a time even for the bullet to get there,	Phrase	Simple/ Suspended
a mysterious, terrible change came over the elephant.	Main Cl.	
He neither stirred	Main Cl.	
nor fell,	Main Cl.	Compound/ Balanced
but every line of his body had altered.	Main Cl.	
He looked suddenly stricken, shrunken, immensely old,	Main Cl.	
as though the frightful impact of the bullet had paralysed him	Sub Cl.	Complex/ Loose
without knocking him down.	Phrase	
At last,	Phrase	
after what seemed a long time	Phrase (inc. Cl.)	
– it might have been five seconds,	(Sub Cl.	Complex/ Suspended
I dare say –	Main Cl.)	
he sagged flabbily	Main Cl.	
to his knees.	Phrase	

(Orwell: *Shooting an Elephant*)

COMMENT

There is a certain amount of repetition within the above
passage – e.g. the opening two Adverbal Preposition-
Phrases; a trio of Adnominal Subject-Complements

'stricken, shrunken, immensely old'. But the elements of repetition occur within a larger variety. The sentences are in order Simple, Compound, and Complex, and they vary in length. All three kinds of movement – Balanced, Loose, Suspended – are represented. There are also a fair number of Preposition Phrases, variously distributed. This variety reflects the complexity of the situation, enabling the writer to bring together a number of elements – the shooting, the 'mysterious change' in the elephant, the attitude and feeling of the observers, etc.

EXERCISES

1. Analyse the following passages similarly to the Sample above. Where possible, indicate any specially effective use either of repetition or of variety of sentence-structure.

a) The uneasy calm did not last. All of a sudden, without the slightest warning, before any precautions could be taken, and to the horror of all on board, the boat turned over and sank.

b) It was an antiquated and very small cinema. Having bought our tickets we had to wait for the girl in the box-office to come out and unlock the doors, so that we could find seats. The same girl tried to help by flashing a torch-light, but the battery was almost dead. When eventually we did sit down, alongside the other half-dozen patrons, we realized that we were in for an unusual experience. The film broke every few minutes, an ancient gramophone played wheezy records while repairs were effected, and in the end the box-office girl announced apologetically that the projector had finally broken down and that we could have our money back.

c) It was the worst traffic-jam I had ever been in, even

on a Bank Holiday. For mile after mile we progressed only in short spurts. The air seemed full of petrol fumes, the engines of the holiday coaches kept up a dull, monotonous throbbing, and from time to time irritated car-drivers sounded their car-horns with futile impatience. Not even the scores of mobile policemen on motor-cycles could get the endless column of traffic moving for more than a few seconds at a time.

2. Analyse similarly any interesting paragraph in a newspaper.

3. Read the following passage several times, aloud and silently, before answering the questions on it.

> I went and stood on the steps leading into the garden. Then I saw them. The locusts.
>
> The air was full of them, made of them. The roof-tops were locusts, the trees and the grass were locusts, the walls were locusts. You felt they were in your very head, behind your eyes.

a) What is significant about the sentence-construction in the first paragraph? What seems to be the writer's purpose?

b) What is the dominant grammatical feature of the second paragraph? Illustrate it in some detail.

4. What is specially noticeable about the sentence structure in:

> The blow was soon to fall. In the dead of night, in the glare and tumult of a summer thunderstorm, two hundred ferocious Indian braves broke into the unhappy village.

Write a similarly constructed pair of sentences such as might appear in a ghost story.

INDEX